COACH to COACH

EMOTIONAL INTELLIGENCE AND LEADERSHIP FOR COACHES

Sara C. Smith

www.CoachtoCoach.info
Starfish Publishing

Coach to Coach: Emotional Intelligence and Leadership For Winning Coaches
Copyright © 2014 by Sara C. Smith
All rights reserved.

Published by:
Starfish Publishing
Fort Worth, TX 76109
817-924-0670
scsmith@slweb.net
Sara C. Smith, MCC, CPCC

Printed in the United States of America
First edition
ISBN: 978-1502865823

Credits

Editor: Kelly Epperson
Cover design and graphics: clark-creative.com, Alison McDonnell
Photography: Locations Photography, Tammy Graham

This is dedicated to the coaches who

feel as though they work alone

struggle in a world that only offers wins and losses as a measure for success

feel enormous pressure to win championships

long for the support of administration or parents or alumni

hunger to create teams of intelligent, respectful young people who have the tools to conquer challenges in the world of competition.

This is also dedicated to those who recognize the life learning possibilities in competitive sports; who see athletics as a place for young people to develop and mature to become responsible adults and who love their field of play for the passion, generosity and respect that can come from great competition.

TABLE OF CONTENTS

ACKNOWLEDGEMENTS

I want to thanks to all those who had faith in me as I wrote *Coach to Coach*. Thanks to David Chow, colleague and friend who sent an athletic coach my way. The opportunity to work in sports has offered some of the most fun I've ever had. Neither of us suspected that one phone call would lead to this!

My heartfelt thanks go to Kyla Holas, Head Softball Coach, University of Houston. Your willingness to step into the unknown of change is a model for others. You are creating a learning environment that builds winning teams and prepares young women to win championships as well as face the challenges of life after college sports. Your willingness to try new ideas gives others courage to make bold changes.

Thanks also to Todd Whitting and his staff at the University of Houston baseball program. You are one of the most practical people I know and are an expert in tough love. You have the talent to see what's possible in athletes and the courage to offer second chances when they are deserved. You put your faith in me to help 'unstick' a few players who were stuck. Watching you get to the Super Regionals was a thrill!

Thanks to Rick Villarreal, Athletic Director at the University of North Texas whose conversations, introductions and support added energy and hope to the journey of this book. And to Tracey Kee (softball) and Sujay Lama (tennis) of UNT who shared stories of how they worked through challenges to emerge as the emotionally intelligent coaches they are. May you continue to develop and inspire young people as you win championships.

Thanks for all the others who offered stories. Your experiences have been invaluable. To those I've already mentioned and let me add Lindsay Vanover, Head Coach, Softball, University of Montevallo.

I want to acknowledge those who have helped get *Coach to Coach* from a folder full of ideas and experiences to published book - especially Kelly Epperson, my editor. You are incredibly patient with all my questions and ready to offer helpful direction. Your thoroughness is reflected in every page. Thanks to friends and colleagues from all walks of my life who took time to read and share ideas: Cindy Charlton, Shan Bates, Chrissy Carew and Katherine Bock. You've given a gift without measure.

Thanks to Alison McDonnell for the graphics and cover design. You captured the spirit of *Coach to Coach* in pictures. Thanks to Tammy Graham, Locations Photography – you are always a creative force and a delight to work with.

Thanks to my coach, Cynthia Loy-Darst. You have challenged, championed and helped me get through the valley of shadows a time or two! Thanks for your unending faith and willingness to look at success in creative ways – as only a coach could! You model and mentor the competencies of our profession brilliantly.

I want to thank Gary Patterson, Head Coach for football at Texas Christian University. In many ways, Coach P has inspired this book by allowing his journey toward emotional intelligence to be public. His candor in speaking about steps and missteps, personal development and change should inspire his players and all the rest of us as he continues building a legacy at TCU.

Finally, to Paul Smith, you are the best. As reader, life and business partner (and so much more), I am enormously grateful. Thanks for your patience when I got into the details of writing so deeply that I had a hard time carrying on a conversation. I couldn't have gotten *Coach to Coach* into the world without you. More to come.

PRE-GAME WARM UP
INTRODUCTION

Coach to Coach is about what is possible when emotional intelligence is at the center of any organization's culture. This book is written for sports coaches – of any game, at any level - because EI is the next level to your success.

Emotional Intelligence is growing in popularity because of the measurable success it brings, and a lot of people are beginning to use it. Since emotional intelligence is becoming a popular bandwagon to jump on, it's important that you know why to start here. First, we will begin with *you* because EI – the shorthand term we'll use for emotional intelligence – can't be *done* to someone else. An organization will only be as emotionally nimble as its leader. The more you operate with healthy emotions, the more your players will become creative, resourceful and resilient. They will become a *team* instead of a group that plays a game together. Conversely, if you are not comfortable or aware of your own emotions, your players will likely be more frantic, less collaborative and more in it for themselves.

In its simplest form, being emotionally intelligent is being able to understand what triggers your emotions so you can begin to control them. Imagine experiencing an event that makes you angry. Only instead of blowing up, you are able to catch yourself and respond calmly. That is emotional intelligence. Being able to corral your impulses leads to the second value of

EI - using your awareness skills to understand and read others' emotional responses so you can work with them more effectively. As you model emotional intelligence for your organization, trust grows more quickly and athletes (and staff) will have the assurance they can safely develop and grow with your support.

The bottom line is an emotionally intelligent organization is one that develops more quickly to become high performance and resilient.

At the core of this book is a hope that every coach in every sport realizes how much their behaviors contribute to the character of their players and the success of the team on many levels. That's why we use a clear approach to teach emotional intelligence and apply it to your environment and the choices you make. I predict that as you practice the skills of emotional intelligence, you will find you have more freedom and better choices.

You'll get insights from what we've learned from EI in business over the past 15 years and what's being taught in some of the best MBA programs. And it's all designed to work for you in the world of athletics. I spent much of my career in IBM helping leaders and executives develop. I've now turned my attention to sports because I know that emotional intelligence will work the same way here.

Whether you are a coach for a university, a middle school or a select team, you can get stuck or frustrated for a lot of different reasons. And the best way to get unstuck and on to greater success, on and off the field, is by taking charge of your emotions.

Coach to Coach provides leadership training tailored for

athletic coaches. You lead a complex organization where some key stakeholders report to you – and many more do not. Even if you are the best coach in your field, if you haven't learned leadership, a big piece of the high performance puzzle is missing. Without training, there is a tendency to lead from your gut – you do what you feel is right or what you've seen other coaches do. Sometimes that works, sometimes it doesn't.

In these pages you'll learn the skills your need to lead responsive teams. You'll find there is as much art and science in leadership as there is in your sport. To know both is to have a true competitive advantage. One of the values I want offer in *Coach to Coach* is the antidote to your job being at risk because of emotional outbursts. There have been too many videos of coaches in mid-rant posted on social media. Whether the outburst was justified or not, those recordings can lead to separations and lawsuits. The lessons of EI are designed to help you stay in control so you can use intensity as a tool without the unpredictability of an emotional explosion.

We will follow a logical progression beginning with learning the basics of emotional intelligence and how apply them. Then we move to skills that will deepen your experience and teach you how to integrate new practices. You will be guided by stories of real coaches and athletes that offer practical examples of how these competencies will work in your world. The names and sports have been modified to make the lessons more universal and because I want you to find yourself, your players and new possibilities in the experiences of others.

At the end of every chapter you will find Practice Drills. They contain steps to integrate new behaviors and then look for the changes in yourself and your organization. You may begin this journey at any time, of course, but I recommend you start when you can give yourself time and space to develop new skills – like the space between the end of one season and the beginning of the next. If you give yourself the opportunity to learn, apply and practice emotional intelligence, I guarantee by the end of Coach to Coach, you will have a toolkit full of new skills.

I have an unflagging belief that the work you do with team sports offers a unique opportunity to create mature, responsible adults. And when you operate from a place of emotional intelligence, you will be even better at it. One thing I've learned working with university head coaches and their teams is that one of the greatest inhibitors to team potential is player immaturity. The gift we can give athletes at any level is the opportunity to mature more quickly, make rational, thoughtful choices and to see beyond the horizon of "what I want right now."

I believe that we can make a significant difference in the world, have fun and enjoy enormous success all at the same time. In *Coach to Coach* I'll show you how. One of the reasons I moved from working in corporations to sports teams is the opportunity to make a difference with young people. I put my philosophy on the back of my business card - "creating the future one leader at a time" - and I invite you to join me playing that bigger game.

Finally, as I was putting the finishing touches on *Coach to Coach*, the news was full of bad behavior in athletics. Professional football players are being indicted for abusing partners, spouses and children. The NFL is floundering to find a way respond. A story broke about a team in New Jersey whose season was cancelled and five varsity players were charged with aggravated sexual assault and criminal restraint

– there was a tradition of brutal hazing. This barbarous approach to athletics where emotional and physical dominance is tolerated and even condoned has to stop. It is not the only way to win. We have the opportunity to redirect the energy of competitive sports from violence to athletic excellence while teaching young people to become emotionally intelligent adults.

By applying what you discover with EI, you can impact your team, your organization, your sport, and the world of athletics. That's no small job but I believe you are up for it. Let's get going.

1

IT BEGINS WITH YOU

*"My responsibility is leadership, and the minute I get
negative, that is going to have an influence on my team."*

Don Shula

The success of your team and your program hinges on you as a
leader.

Notice I didn't say it hinged on you as a "coach." There isn't any
question that expertise in your sport is extremely important,
but your skill as a leader is just as critical. Because unless your
situation is different from many coaches I've met, you are
leading a pretty complex organization.

The irony is that as a coach, you have many opportunities to
learn about the game; new equipment, drills for players or the
latest in strategy. What's often missing is the opportunity to
learn the art and science of leadership. I'm not suggesting
gaining the level you'd get with an MBA, but to learn the nuts
and bolts of leading a healthy organization. How do you
respond when a player thinks he doesn't have to work hard
because he's gotten the scholarship? Or the parent who is
ready to take every grievance to your athletic director. Or any

of the countless issues that aren't a part of the game but can take so much time!

Solid leadership from the coach is critical to success in sports, because what ultimately delivers success in any program is not the equipment or facilities or funds. It's *people*. And people, programs and teams need leadership.

So where do you begin to develop as a leader? Sure, you can start by emulating others, but you want to choose the right people to model. And once you choose, what exactly do you look for? How do you recognize great leadership in sports?

I suspect you've known coaches who had a profound, positive affect on the programs they've created. And it's possible that you've experienced the impact of great leadership in your life and career. But that doesn't answer the question – where can I learn leadership? *Coach to Coach* is designed to help by providing insights into what it takes to be a true leader and how you get there. We will look at the science of leadership, best practices and behaviors that are easy to learn. You will get tools and exercises to help you on your journey to becoming a great leader for your organization.

You'll learn that leadership isn't inborn – that you either have it or you don't. Leadership is made up of measurable behaviors - skills that can be learned. Leadership is as much science as it is art and I'm going to bring that science out of the pages of corporate leadership and MBA courses to you right here, right now. You have the advantage my close to forty years of leadership experience offered in a concise, sports-centric form.

When I began in business, leadership was all about "command and control." It was a leadership style holdover from all the officers who came back from World War II. They stepped out of uniform and into leadership positions and control-through-giving-orders became the default. Then corporations began to evolve because strategies shifted from products being their competitive advantage to *people* being their most valuable asset. As strategies changed, leadership evolution had to follow. I worked as part of the IBM transformation team that took on the challenge to shift and strengthen leadership to pull the company from the brink of corporate collapse. We were successful and IBM was re-invented.

What I learned about leadership there will work for you. Athletics have a lot in common with IBM. The corporate landscape is as competitive as any sport - just with different uniforms!

As a professional coach and transformation consultant at IBM, I learned about emotional intelligence from some of the greatest minds in behavioral science. I've been using those skills to help leaders apply effective leadership and high performance teaming to their organizations ever since. Working with coaches and their teams has allowed me to combine my skills of leadership development with my love of sports in both my work and this book.

I've learned what works, what doesn't and how to translate business experience to the youth-oriented, high-octane world of amateur sports. We are going to build on the shoulders of what's been learned in business to bring the advantages of emotionally intelligent leadership into your arena quickly to help you develop a new competitive advantage.

You'll learn leadership through the stories of coaches and their teams and walk through the steps to bring emotionally intelligent leadership and positive results to you entire organization. My job is to give you the tools you need to develop a winning game plan for success. Your job is to be open to change – because the success of your program begins with you.

When I say we are going to dive into the depths of leadership, I am referring to the "people side" of your work. You will discover the lessons of leadership in ways that are personal and drawn from real stories. The practices you'll get within these pages are proven, practical and doable in your world. You can think of this as part of your playbook.

Your organization is a reflection of you. How you influence others begins with what motivates you and what you value. Your team draws their behavioral clues from what they hear you say and see you do. The values you model will become a key component of your team's culture.

One of our first goals is to increase your awareness of your own actions as seen through the lens of how you impact others. The first step is to help you become intentional – to be clear in what you want and then develop a culture to reflect it. A high performance organization is rarely built on unexamined, default behaviors.

What is critical is for you to become aware and intentional of what you are communicating. If you believe you are pretty balanced between the two – the game and the people - that's a great start. If not, take a couple of days and note what's foremost in your thoughts and conversations. Notice what your words and behaviors are communicating to your organization. Do you spend more time on the game or the players? Is it easier to focus on the work? All of these are clues to what has your attention. You have to decide what you want to create. If you aren't clear about your destination, you can easily choose the wrong path.

Here's what I mean, meet Ben.

Ben had just started his dream job. He was coming into the position as one of the youngest head coaches ever hired into a nationally acclaimed basketball program. He had been a star player for the team several years earlier. His alma mater, now his employer, had always been admired for the quality of its program and when the longtime head coach announced his retirement, Ben knew he wanted the job.

His enthusiasm has been just what they were looking for and Ben was brought in as the up-and-coming star head coach. He had been a great asset as a player and the administration anticipated that his understanding of the program's history would ensure he would uphold its legacy – they saw him as a natural extension of their past successes. Maintaining consistency in the existing program would make him successful.

But Ben had other ideas. He wanted to make it HIS program. He was young and creative and ready to "shake things up."

Turns out, Ben was the complete package – almost. He knew the game inside and out. He was a great strategist and had been an outstanding team captain. What was missing in him was an understanding of the human complexity that surrounds an athletic program: the administration, staff, alumni, donors, players, parents and fans. The view turned out to be very different on the other side of the ball!

Our formerly great player overlooked the most important element of this new game he had been hired to play - the "people" side of running an organization.

Ben hit the ground running. He believed he could build on his prowess as a player to become a championship coach. Being hired over a field of qualified older coaches felt like an endorsement that gave him license to make all the changes he saw fit to mold the program and make it his own.

He jumped into imposing changes with the administrative support team in his second week. Ben reassigned people, re-arranged furniture and even had people change offices and responsibilities. He made demands about what he wanted done and by when.

He never took the time to see how the existing processes worked. He figured he knew enough from when he was there before. After all, it was largely the same office staff that had been around when he was in the program as a student. And with a wave of his wand, Ben created chaos out of order...and left discontent and resistance in his wake.

He was so busy rearranging everything about the team that he failed to notice that the newly retired head coach hadn't actually left. The previous coach and the athletic director were buddies and the AD told his retiring friend that he would always be welcome! So when the team showed up for their first workout, the new coach Ben was on the court and the former coach was sitting up in the stands.

Either "too much too soon" or the unspoken strength of the old guard could spell trouble for the new coach. In fact, all sorts of alarms should have gone off in his head but Ben was oblivious. There were a couple of other items Ben missed. He didn't realize it was "smart ball" to establish a new relationship with the athletic director. This time it should be as the new head basketball coach, not a former player. He also failed to see the importance of meeting key alumni, supporters and donors. Instead, he simply put his head down and worked on the game.

To net out Ben's mistake, he thought success was only about the game of basketball, so he focused on those results. All of his attention was on the logistics and details of getting ready for a new season. You couldn't fault him for effort, he worked hard to execute his game plan. The problem was, he wasn't aware – Ben just didn't pay attention to the feelings of others. It wasn't a surprise that he missed the rumblings that were beginning. His lack of awareness led him to his next blunders.

Ben felt everyone else should be working as hard as he was and he never missed an opportunity to make sure everyone knew. Cynical comments like "Leaving already?" and "Oh, did you decide to sleep in this morning?" were common. He was blind to his insensitivity and didn't notice or seem to care about his impact. He demanded compliance and bullied anyone who didn't meet his standards...after all, it was all in the name of the game.

Ben's demands for excellence (and intolerance of nothing less) touched everyone from janitors to staff and players. As one of the youngest head coaches ever hired, he was settling into the belief that it gave him license to "be in charge."

Ben unwittingly failed at almost every turn. This personable, talented athlete-turned-coach managed to offend almost everyone and all because he wasn't aware of the impact he was having. He had the potential to be a great coach, but the organization was grinding to a halt under Ben's leadership (or lack thereof) because everyone - secretaries, trainers and support staff - felt as though they were second-class citizens.

The retired coach watched with amusement from the background. And since Ben had never approached him to create a new relationship, Former Coach defaulted to looking at him as a player who had "gotten too big for his britches." Former Coach felt free to commiserate and share his opinions with all of his old buddies – the administration, fans and alumni. And since Ben had not reached out to establish his own relationship with any of those groups, he was left on the outside looking in. He became an interloper - people saw Ben as the upstart who thought he knew everything.

He was failing – not because of his work with the game. He was brilliant at the game. Ben was failing because of all he was overlooking. He was oblivious to the discontent he was creating and by the time he realized it, it was too late.

Ben only lasted two years and was shocked when he was fired. It wasn't until he worked with a professional business coach and learned about emotional intelligence that he was able to understand what had derailed him.

What Ben learned – and what we'll explore - is the impact of emotional intelligence in sports coaching.

When we look at Ben's actions from a pure athletic coaching

perspective, his approach seemed reasonable. He had been a successful player and loved the game. He realized he had a knack for analysis and strategy. The next logical step was to become a coach.

Think about why you became a coach. If you have a talent for developing players and an ability to see what others might miss on the playing field, shouldn't that be enough to be a great coach? As we learned from Ben's story, the answer to that question is a resounding NO.

Being unaware or uncaring about the impact you are having can lead to your downfall – as it was for Ben. As his story teaches us, the game is different on the coach's side of the ball (or puck). That's where our work together begins. We will start with the fact that you know how to coach your sport and fill in what you want to know about leadership.

A winning game plan has three steps. First, you will become more aware and intentional in your leadership. As you model emotional intelligence (EI), your athletes will begin to learn emotional stability from you. That will allow them to remove their emotional obstacles and reach higher levels of athletic performance more quickly. That's the second step. Finally, your new coaching skills will help you lead the entire organization to become resilient – from top to bottom. These are ambitious goals but doable, if you are willing to play.

In the next chapters, you will get the fundamentals of high performance leadership and ways to implement them quickly and effectively. I'll provide explanations, examples and practical ways to apply what you learn. At the end of every chapter, you will be offered a practice drill. You will also find space to journal...to make notes about your experiences. I encourage you to take time to jot them down so when you get to the end of the book, you'll be able to recall your "ah-ha's." They will help reinforce your learning.

The practice drills can be approached like a player's practice routine. Each is designed to help you test-drive the muscles of good leadership. You'll learn the emotional intelligence basics – in the same way you teach fundamentals to your players. Just take them one step at a time. Every new stage of development will build on what you've just practiced.

What has been said in countless locker rooms is true — what you do in practice shows up in the game. It's the same here. By now you are continuing to read because you want more – or you are curious. I'm glad to join you on your journey. Congratulations on having the courage to change. The most successful sports coaches will be those who boldly go...

So let's get started.

PRACTICE DRILLS

The practice for this chapter is in preparation to learn about emotional intelligence. This is the skill of becoming aware – of *noticing*.

Spend the next day noticing your default pace and habits. For example –

- Do you eat breakfast on the run or do you make time to sit down and eat each day?

- Do you find yourself checking your smartphone while someone's talking to you?

- Do you find yourself wondering where the last hour went?

- Are you always early for you next appointment or do you run late?

- Do you find yourself finishing other's sentences so the conversation goes faster?

- Do you give yourself time in the day to plan for what's coming or debrief what's just occurred?

Log your activities, what gets accomplished and what doesn't, who helps you and who gets left out.

Slow down, notice and take note.

journal page

2

EMOTIONAL INTELLIGENCE – YOUR COMPETITIVE ADVANTAGE

"No matter what leaders set out to do...their success depends on how they do it. Even if they get everything else just right, if leaders fail in this primal task of driving emotions in the right direction, nothing they do will work as well as it could or should."

Primal Leadership, Goleman, Boyatzis, McKee

As we learned from Ben's story, success in coaching is more than just being good at the game. The abilities you have in your sport – your knowledge of strategy, rules and execution – are only part of your toolkit. Our next step will be to show how emotional intelligence (EI) is an equally critical success factor.

We are going to look at four ideas in this chapter -

- See why emotional intelligence is relevant in sports
- Determine EI can make your team more competitive
- Learn new leadership skills to replace "command and control"
- Keep old (bad) habits from ruling you

Let's begin with how EI is relevant in sports. What you will find in athletics is not so different from what we see in business - where the study of emotional intelligence began. Business executives will tell you that 80 percent or more of the challenges they face are not in products or processes. Their greatest challenges are people problems. Sound familiar?

You've seen it in your world. We're talking about the idiosyncrasies of the players – or their parents, maybe a headstrong assistant coach or a pushy front office administrator. It seems that every time people are added to the elegance of any game, things get complicated. How do you cope? And is coping the best you can do?

The value of being an emotionally intelligent leader is that you are able to work through differences and unexpected interruptions with grace rather than emotional explosions. You'll see that coping is **not** the best you can expect. You will learn to create an environment where trust and open communications become the norm– where you and everyone in your organization can thrive.

One word of caution: there are a growing number of people who are introducing EI into the world of sports. Many of them focus on what you should teach your athletes. That is not the best place to begin. The truth is, an emotionally intelligent organization must begin with you - at the top. Until the leader (or coach) is on board, understands, lives and embraces EI, there won't be much progress. That's the caution. You really can't to "do" emotional intelligence to others. You must experience it and be willing to its behaviors.

Since you set the tone and direction, an EI shift must begin with you. If you apply yourself to the lessons here, I predict that by the time you choose to implement programs for your athletes, you will already be seeing the positive results that occur when EI is a cornerstone of an organization. We learned it in business and it's true in sports – sustainable change begins at the top.

A good example of the importance of behavior at the top of an organization is the downfall of Enron, the Houston, Texas energy giant. The organization became a reflection of its leaders. Enron executives thought nothing of using accounting loopholes, in fact, it was a matter of practice. Senior executives routinely misrepresented the company to their board, stockholders and customers. Their misguided values – cutting corners and shortchanging the truth - became the norm. The downfall of Enron (and their accounting firm, Arthur Andersen) was the result. Enron may seem like an extreme example, but its story demonstrates how culture permeates an organization. Equally dysfunctional cultures can occur in sports, too. We'll look at some examples later on.

Since emotional intelligence is a term being bandied about by a lot of people, let's make sure we are using the same definition. I'll turn to Dr. Daniel Goleman, one of the foremost authorities of EI who defines emotional intelligence as "the capacity for recognizing our own feelings and those of others, for motivating ourselves and for managing emotions well in ourselves and in our relationships."

When we look at Ben's story through the lens of Goleman's definition, we see how Ben completely overlooked the feelings of others. Since I used the term *feelings*, let's be clear on that, too. If you are tempted to dismiss the subject of feelings as too "touchy-feely," you're not alone. The command and control approach of leading typically shies away from considering the human element - by that I mean peoples' feelings. When leaders rely solely on telling people what to do, they aren't concerned with workers' reactions - only compliance. Let's be honest, it feels easier – less risky. However, there is a downside. Command and control is most effective in a world of repetitive tasks where a worker checks in, build widgets all day and then leaves. The problem is what leaders gain in compliance they lose when they quash peoples' creativity, innovation and initiative.

We learned in business that, comfortable or not, emotions are a driving motivator. If dealing with them makes you a little uneasy, don't worry. Emotions are typically uncomfortable when we aren't prepared to handle them, so my job is to help you be ready.

In fact, you'll find that what were seen as soft skills - touchy-feely - 15 years ago are now recognized as complex relationship skills. They are the ones you'll be learning in this book. I've created a roadmap to help you understand and practice emotional intelligence so you can replace discomfort with confidence.

Back to Ben for a moment. Part of his problem was that he was totally focused on the game and ignored the people side of the equation. Add to that, he was also emotionally invested in doing things his way. That kept him blind to the impact he was having on others. Goleman was talking to the Bens of the world when he said, "If your emotional abilities aren't in hand, if you don't have self-awareness, if you are not able to manage your emotions, if you can't have empathy and have effective relationships, then no matter how smart you are, you are not going to get very far."

That sets the stage. Now let's build the framework of the importance of EI for coaches.

First, your organization is as complex as any in the corporate world. As you consider your constituencies (staff, players, supports, financial supporters, administration, etc.) think of the roles you must play. You are required to be collaborator, diplomat, spokesperson and emotional guide. That's a lot of hats for one person. They are the same hats top executives wear. And just as executives need to learn the art and science of leadership, so do smart coaches.

We've learned several things in business over the past 15 years that will jumpstart your effectiveness. First, the best leaders recognized the connection between how they treat their employee and productivity. We know that motivated people make the best workers. It's the same in sports. There is a strong connection between emotionally intelligent leadership and workers' (or players', in your world) motivation.

In the beginning, emotional intelligence was only leadership theory. Then sophisticated MRI's (magnetic resonance imaging) came on the scene and we were able to map brain activity and could see impact of emotions on response and motivation. Social neuroscience, the study of stimuli and brain response, showed us the physical impact of emotional intelligence. It provided scientific evidence that effective leadership was tied to our ability to control our own emotions and influence the emotions of those we lead. More on that later.

In sports, your emotional intelligence is foundational to building your organization's resilience. Dr. Richard Boyatzis, another authority in EI tells us, "We find that most of the characteristics that differentiate the outstanding performers from the rest of the field are these things that we call social and emotional competencies."

Boyatzis specifically used the word *competencies* because the definition of a competency is a behavior and behaviors can be learned. That's good news – emotional intelligence is made up of learnable skills.

To make sure we are on the same page, *behavior* means what we do, what we say and how we react. When I talk about the impact someone is having, that's what we look for. One of the most hopeful messages we take from all the emerging brain research is the fact that our brains continue to grow and expand. We can learn new things until the day we die. The old wives' tale of not being able to change as we grow older is a myth. Old dogs (and that includes all of us) *can* learn new tricks!

The message? It's not only your expertise as a coach or your knowledge of your sport that are keys to your success. You want to go the next step - to be an emotionally intelligent leader. The bottom line is unless you understand yourself; it's almost impossible to recognize how your emotions are affecting you. And if you can't see the impact of your own emotions, it's virtually impossible to recognize the impact you are having on others. Remember Ben's story – he was running on emotional autopilot – oblivious and uncaring. He had virtually no hint of his negative impact until it was too late.

Another value of practicing good emotional intelligence is that emotions are contagious. When you successfully model emotional intelligence, your team will learn to respond to stressful game situations without blowing up or falling apart.

This skill is called resilience. Resilience takes practice and as you and your organization are able to recognize, manage and use emotions, you will hold a competitive advantage over the teams that don't. As a top coach and leader, you want that competitive advantage. There's a long-term payoff, too. As your team becomes more emotionally resilient, they will be better prepared to meet the emotionally charged, unpredictable world that waits for them as they leave your program.

I don't know where you are in your leadership journey and I'm not here to condemn any approach. It could be that you've spent much of your career in the traditional "command and control" method of coaching. Many coaches grew up experiencing and emulating an authoritarian approach and it's worked in the past. What you'll learn in *Coach to Coach* isn't designed to replace everything you've known. Our goal is to expand your range and choices by increasing the number of tools in your coaching toolkit.

One thing you will be asked to do in is become aware of your default styles and reactions. There will be practice drills at the end of each chapter designed to help you test drive new skills and alternatives, then assess the outcomes.

Our first goal will be to eliminate (or at least minimize) uncontrolled emotions because they are obstacles to leading a high performing team. You'll learn how effective leadership is as much about what you model to the team as what you say.

When you manage emotions in yourself, you will lead your team to more emotional control. Unmanaged emotions are some of the most debilitating barriers to a team's performance. When you take the drama out of the equation of team sports and replace it with clarity and stability, you'll free your athletes to play their game. I want to be clear. Increasing emotional intelligence won't guarantee your team will win championships, but you will find that a team with their emotions under control is better equipped to play to the utmost of their athletic abilities.

Let's pull all these concepts together. People in organizations reflect the leader's emotions. Therefore, responsibility for an organization's effectiveness lives at the top with its leader. That is not new news – but it underlines the fact that it all begins with you. What may be new is that if you improve your emotional intelligence, your organization's climate will improve. Once you are on a path to EI behaviors, you will be able to instill emotionally intelligent behaviors in your team.

Emotionally intelligent leadership and high performance organizations go hand in hand. When you create a vibrant, sustainable organization, you can change assistants or graduate a class of star players and the team will continue its high performance culture without missing a step. Teams really do reflect the leadership at the top - great organizations don't happen by accident.

One of the areas of sports that's important for us to address is the relationship between emotional intelligence and competition. Competition presents an enormous paradox in sports: it is necessary, the essence of sports. And at the same time, competition has a dark side – one that shows up when we talk about things like crushing the competition. Just the term *competition* has taken on more than one meaning. It is the act of two teams engaging in a contest, the energy of the contest or the team we are playing.

There are many directions a discussion about competition

might take, but for our purposes, we are going to focus on the *energy* of competition. We will look at how it affects you and how you use it to motivate others. We're also going to look at the ways competition can impact an organization in terms of values and ethics.

We'll start by examining ways competition motivates coaches. For example, how do you experience competition – how does it affect you? Do you find you want to win, no matter the cost? I spoke with one coach who did. He valued the win more than players and told me his job was to weed out the weak and put the strong on the field. You can hear the heartless nature of competition echo in that philosophy. He had a relentless focus on winning that left discarded players in his wake. It's an attitude that thinly veils cruelty. By the way, I suspect it only works in environments where there is an unending source of talent.

The energy of competition can be so ingrained in us that it can show up in surprising places - like driving down the freeway. We care because competition can be an emotionally triggering event that doesn't work in a coach's favor. I'll explain how and show you alternatives. When competition works for you, it's a powerful tool. When it works against you, it can be debilitating.

We'll begin by understanding the power of unquestioned competitive urges. Unexamined emotions can run our lives without our realizing it. Take a moment to ponder these questions -

- When am I aware of being competitive?

- Am I being competitive at times when I'm not aware of it?

- How much do I manage competition and how much does it manage me?"

- Has there ever been a time, in the heat of battle (or a game that's on the line), that I've crossed a line and later wished I hadn't? (It could have been something like yelling at a player, an official or someone in the crowd.)

These are meant to be challenging questions. They point to the risks of being driven by unquestioned competition.

We've seen this face of uncontrolled competition in the picture of the coach nose to nose with a player, yelling at the top of her lungs or during an interview at the end of a heartbreaking loss when a comment comes out that a coach wishes he could take back. Sadly, we've seen coaches fired because of throwing something at a heckling fan or abusing a player.

The important question is, have you ever been so overwhelmed by the need to win that you've considered – or exhibited - behaviors that trump good sense and self-control? It can happen in a heartbeat. Unbridled emotions can show up in a lot of ways, from verbal abuse to physical violence. And if the occasional slip isn't enough to be concerned about, thanks to the proliferation of smart phones and social media, we get to see recordings of coaches losing control posted on the web for the world to see and share.

Recall the 2013 video of Mike Rice, Rutgers men's basketball coach. In the recording, that went viral, he berated his players and used stereotypical slurs while kicking and throwing balls. It led to his firing. I don't know Mike Rice and assume there is a lot more to the story than just the damning video. The point is, in a high stress, highly competitive environment, blow-ups happen.

Can you think of a time something compromising happened to you? If the answer is yes, take heart. Emotions are human reactions and if you slipped, you are not alone. Part of what we want to do is create the self-awareness and self-management to keep emotional tsunamis from occurring in your future.

One more caution – in some cases, we'll be pushing back on some long-held athletic traditions. For example, have you ever heard anyone declare, "Winning isn't everything, it's the only thing!"?

It may sound inspirational on the surface. In fact, it might be a line you've used with a team that's lost its concentration and needs to get their heads back in the game. But there's another message beneath those words that is neither subtle nor ethical: winning is so important it will justify any means to get there. Wow, let's see how that can get out of hand!

- Southern Methodist University received the NCAA death penalty in 1986 for a wide spread (also widely known and accepted) practice of offering favors and financial advantage. *Whatever it takes!*

- The New Orleans Saints head football coach, Sean Payton, was suspended for a year because his defensive players received monetary bounties for hurting players on the opposing teams' offenses. *Winning is the only thing!*

It's not just limited to football –

- The Baylor University basketball coach was fired after one player murdered another and the coach advised players to lie to the NCAA about the circumstances, players and drugs. Once uncovered, even more violations were revealed. *Whatever it takes.*

Winning is NOT the only thing.

These examples are the ones that make the headlines. But it's important to also be aware of grey areas. They are smaller, but no less important examples of lapses in ethical behavior that can be invited through a singular focus on winning.

In softball, it could be the illegal pitch, where the pitcher's foot comes off the ground. After all, many umpires don't call it more than once or twice in a game. In football, it could be an illegal block in the back or hitting a quarterback a little hard or a little late. My favorite example was one I saw in an Olympic water polo match. These superb aquatic athletes would pull one another underwater using only their legs and then hold up their hands trying to look innocent – in clear violation of the rules.

"Whatever it takes" clouded the judgment of players in Major League Baseball in what's now known as the Baseball Steroids Era. In cycling, Lance Armstrong was the unprecedented winner of seven Tours du France until he was disqualified from all the races and banned from competitive cycling for life for doping offenses.

Part of the challenge is that in some circles, some of these behaviors become expected. But the "everyone does it" mentality is only an excuse. Let's call them what they are – examples of cheating. And for the record, even though they were lauded in the short term, some of the darlings of their sports, Mark McGuire, Lance Armstrong, Alex Rodriguez and others, often end up censured or disgraced.

Our interest is in how this cycle begins so we can help stop it. How does a great athlete or great coach come to believe that questionable behavior is acceptable? It's that moment when the fever pitch of competition invites a good coach to declare, "Winning isn't everything, it's the only thing." As you've seen (and maybe experienced) unchecked emotions can become a slippery slope.

I want you to be aware of one more unforeseen impact of competition that shaped a coach's life. Here is what happened

A successful college softball coach, Sandy, had been the winning pitcher in a championship game when she was a student. It was a marathon of a game that lasted over twenty innings. As a 20-year-old player, the lesson she took away about competition was "no sacrifice is too great." It had taken tremendous physical sacrifice just to make it through the game. Sandy had pushed her physical limits to stay in the game while her opponents tired and were replaced. She was the hero and unquestioned sacrifice became her standard for being competitive moving forward.

Years later as a coach, her no-sacrifice-too-great perspective was still alive and well. But it was no longer working. She found out that others didn't understand her definition of commitment. When one of her players would tire and "give up", first Sandy would be baffled then she became angry. Sandy's anger was triggered by what she saw as the athlete's lack of commitment. She simply couldn't understand why they didn't care enough. Why wouldn't today's student athletes commit to perform as she had?

What she didn't realize is that her motivation was her own. Commitment and response to competitive pressures are personal. Each player had her own self-imposed pressures. Their motivations were different than hers and Sandy learned that few were competitive in the same way as she.

Sandy had not realized she was demanding more than people would – or could – deliver. Until she became emotionally intelligent and learned how to notice, she wasn't aware of the impact of her uncompromising requirements. When people didn't meet her expectations, she would get angry. Her anger was dark, intense and frightening. It would flare if Sandy thought an athlete was holding back. Once triggered, her behaviors were dictated by emotion rather than rational thought. It was creating a red flag situation - that's when a coach is capable of responding in ways they might later regret.

One value of emotional intelligence is to uncover and defuse volatile competitive responses that might be unrealized. That's what Sandy did. She was able to respond differently once she realized what was happening and why. When she chose to respond differently, she was able to treat each athlete uniquely and create trust instead of fear. Her story teaches the foundations of emotional intelligence. First there was self-awareness that led to self-management.

One of the most valuable skills to take with you is the ability to recognize your emotions so that you can manage them. That will allow you to act rather than react when things get tough. Like our softball-star-turned-coach, you may discover unexamined behaviors that could threaten to undermine what you want to create. The more your self-awareness grows, the more you will be able to reinvent yourself as a coach – keeping what serves you and replacing what does not.

I share stories like Sandy, Ben and others so you can learn from their experiences. If you are able to begin to recognize triggers and manage emotions that could threaten your success, you'll have a strong foundation to create emotional intelligence.

A dozen years ago I moved from a leadership position in IBM to training leaders. I had an executive call emotional intelligence "California woo-woo." He refused to have any part of it and his team suffered through his lack of awareness. You are already ahead of him in understanding because you have the benefit of knowing that it is neither fluff nor woo-woo. It is proven social neuroscience. What seemed "soft" before is now recognized as complex human relationship skills. Once you begin to practice them, you'll find it is pretty hard-core stuff.

Game on.

PRACTICE DRILLS

Building Self-Awareness

Recognize how emotions can get out of control.

Consider the stories of coaches who have had public or private meltdowns (like Mike Rice, the Rutgers basketball coach who was fired for abuse). Your assignment is to ponder these questions and make some notes:

- What was the coach trying to communicate with the outburst?

- What message was received?

- What was the impact on the players and organization in the short term and the long term (did things get better or worse)?

- What was the benefit of their actions?

- What was the cost?

Become aware of the power of competition in yourself.

This is an exercise of awareness, not judgment. No one is keeping score. Take a day and be aware of your energy – how it ebbs and flows. Here are some places to look –

- Do you find driving on a freeway to be a competitive event?

- If one of your assistant coaches suggests a practice routine you know nothing about, what is your response?

- When you see an athlete doing some wrong, what is your response? For example, is your first response to demonstrate how to do it right?

journal page

3

EMOTIONAL INTELLIGENCE: THE STATS OF SUCCESS

"It is very important to understand that emotional intelligence is not the opposite of intelligence, it is not the triumph of heart over head - it is the unique intersection of both."

David Caruso, *Emotional What?*

There's been a lot written about emotional intelligence and the importance of the mental game in sports. There are so many opinions I think it's a good idea for us to get in sync. We'll take this chapter to learn the basics of emotional intelligence. Think of this like the beginning of a sports clinic where the leader sets the stage so participants know what they will be learning. We'll set the stage for the changes you'll be practicing later by defining emotional intelligence and how we will use it.

To begin the journey, let's look at the meaning of words -

- *Emotional* is having to do with feelings – anger, fear and happiness

- *Intelligence* is being able to recognize, reason and make choices

I think it's easiest to learn the elements of emotional intelligence when we look at them as a picture.

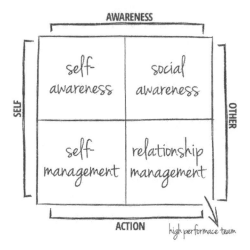

It was Daniel Goleman who spoke about the relationship of the four terms I've place in the quadrants, calling them the elements of emotional intelligence. The graphic provides a visual representation of the elements and how they interrelate. We'll look at it as a whole and then examine each square in more detail. This is the foundation for building emotional intelligence.

We begin with the two squares that create a column on the left. They are labeled SELF - Self-Awareness and Self-Management and represent how an individual's emotions move from awareness to action. The column on the right is labeled OTHER. Those squares represent how we see and work with others – Social Awareness and Relationship Management.

The rows are also identified. The top row is AWARENESS - knowing our self and understanding others. The bottom row is ACTION – how we manage ourselves and how we manage our relationships with others.

So buckle up and let's get started by stepping through the model.

Emotional intelligence always starts with **Self-Awareness**.

That's the ability to understand our own emotions and how they impact us. Self-awareness is fundamental to emotional intelligence because we can only manage what we recognize. Let's meet Tom, his story shows how unexamined emotions impact performance.

> *Tom was a great college catcher. In fact, his coach believed that he was destined for the major leagues. The problem was that by the third game in a weekend series, Tom had run out of gas. He worked so hard in the first two games that by the time he got to Sunday afternoon, his tank was empty. When he was tired, he made mental mistakes and his sloppy play led to losses. To make matters worse, once the mistakes started, Tom would get so angry with himself that what little energy he had left was wasted on anger.*
>
> *His problems began with the fear of not doing well and escalated to anger with himself when his play began to*

deteriorate. Tom didn't realize that emotions were running his life and putting his position and professional aspirations in jeopardy.

It might be easy to jump to what seems to be the obvious emotional diagnosis – Tom should control his anger. After all, when games began to get out of hand, he got angry and lost control. That's what his coach assumed, but he and Tom weren't making any headway correcting the issue. I was called in to work with Tom and we discovered his initial emotion wasn't anger, it was fear - the fear of not being good enough. When that fear triggered him, it cascaded emotions that ended up with his becoming unmanageably angry with himself.

Let me pause to explain the idea of emotional triggers. It's one of the most helpful concepts in understanding self-awareness. A trigger can be any event that creates an emotional response. So with Tom, we looked for what triggered his anger. As we talked, I learned he wanted two things: first, to be the field general from his position as catcher. Second was to look good for the pro scouts. Those are good goals, but they were creating an emotional minefield for Tom. His first trigger was the pressure of looking good and performing well. Any small mistake would be magnified by performance anxiety and that would lead to becoming angry.

Tom would get triggered early in the 3-game series and experience an amygdala hijack – I'll explain that in a minute. The outcome was tension that led to overcompensation that led to the anger all because he wasn't aware of his emotions or how to manage them. By the way, emotions aren't bad unless they are out of control. They are just another type of information. The more we are aware of triggers, the more we are able to manage emotions and allow ourselves access to the information they offer.

We'll get back to Tom, but let's get you involved in the skill of self-awareness – that will help you understand your triggers so you can move to the next step in the model.

Take a moment and think of a game official you experienced who was sloppy. For example, go back to a time when an official cost your team an important game. Remember what you experienced when he or she didn't make a crucial call – like a marginal call that didn't go your way and changed the outcome of the game.

Get your experience in mind then stop and notice how you are feeling right now. If you allow yourself to go back and touch the memory, you can actually begin to feel the same tension begin to build in your body. By the way, tension can show up in a lot of places. You might notice a knot in your stomach or tightness in your shoulders or perhaps pressure behind your eyes.

It doesn't matter where you notice tension building – each of us has our own stress center. What's important is that you recognize where it begins for you. Once you are aware of your physical response to emotions – your trigger – you have the opportunity to manage it. This noticing exercise is one you can repeat until you recognize when and where emotions spark a physical response in you. It's the first step toward self-awareness.

The event we just walked through - thinking about that inept official – is called a trigger event. The trigger invited an emotional response.

Notice how just mentioning a lousy official in your past can create tension. The power of emotions is significant. I simply invited you to recall a memory and the connection brought back strong emotions. Positive emotions work the same way. When you connect with a strong pleasant experience (a wedding day, birth of a child, getting a coveted scholarship) you'll experience those emotions through recollection, as well. The importance of understanding the power of emotions becomes clear. If you can experience an emotional response through a mere suggestion, so can anyone on your team, your staff or in the bleachers.

The more you understand, the more prepared you will be to deal with emotions. The heart of emotional intelligence is self-knowing.

Before we move on, let's look at the science of an emotional response– the amygdala hijack. Here's how it works. Tom's fear of not looking good started his hijack. The adrenaline rush of competition began early in the first game and quickly became a flood of stress chemicals. The more Tom ran in that high gear of emotions, the more he depleted his stock of energy. If he had only understood what was occurring at the beginning of his emotional roller coaster, he might have been able to moderate his response. Instead, he became the victim of an amygdala hijack.

Amygdala hijack is a term coined by Daniel Goleman in his book *Emotional Intelligence.* The amygdala is the emotional control of the brain that regulates our fight, flight or freeze response. When humans experience something that is threatening, the amygdala takes over. When it does, stress hormones flood the body with a chemical cocktail that speeds up the heart and sets a series of physical responses in motion that redirects blood flow to the hands and feet – so we can be ready for battle or to run for the hills.

It's a defensive response that is as old as humankind. Our challenge today is that the amygdala hasn't evolved since prehistoric times. That's why we refer to it as the "reptilian" part of our brain. The amygdala takes stress (like wanting to perform well or reacting to a referee's call) and translates it into a personal threat. The threat response served us well when saber tooth tigers roamed the world. Back then peril required an immediate response from the amygdala. We had to act and act quickly.

Today, the amygdala's threat response can take over an unaware brain in a heartbeat, which is only an asset if you are facing an actual dangerous situation. But it's the 21st century and threats take very different forms and an amygdala hijack may not be the best way to respond. Remember, the amygdala creates a flood of chemicals that course through the body to do a handful of things. They speed up the heart, narrow our visual and mental focus and force much of the blood supply to our hands and feet – to facilitate "fight or flight or freeze."

One important side effect of extreme emotions to know is that they make it more difficult to think clearly. It makes sense because when your blood supply is redirected away from your brain it takes the oxygen with it. Oxygen is essential for clear thinking. The less oxygenated the brain, the less effectively it functions.

Think of a time you've gotten so angry that you responded before you could think. It can happen far too easily in sports and with dire consequences. We don't have to look any further than coaches who throw things. That's an amygdala hijack in action. We should not be naïve enough to think that it can never happen to us. Emotions happen – it's part of being human. And strong emotions are always waiting on the sidelines in competitive sports because our games provide a modern day version of a battle.

There is one other byproduct of an amygdala hijack that's good to know. Once we are in full hijack, the chemicals and their effects stay in our bodies for four to six hours – even up to a full day. You've likely felt the tension after a heartbreaking game for several hours. Every time you recalled the game, the feelings washed over you like it had just happened. Even now, if you think of that impossible referee you may experience the bitter anger begin to rise again.

In many respects, an amygdala hijack is a diabolical gift that keeps on giving. Think of Tom or your team after a heart-breaking loss. If the emotional hijacks are not handled, there is no easy way to overcome what happens in our bodies. The effects can impact the next game of a double header or the play later in a tournament.

We'll talk about the relevance of timing later, but it's important to note that the brain's neural pathway to ignite the amygdala is normally a six to eight millisecond trip. The route to the frontal cortex, the rational part of the brain, takes about 40 milliseconds. The job of emotional intelligence is to give you time to countermand default emotional reactions. Our highly effective survival response is helpful if there is a physical threat – like that saber toothed tiger or a mugger on a subway. But when the perceived threat is wanting to perform well and not measuring up or being at the mercy of an inept game official, the radical stress response is not helpful.

I'll be the first to confess that my explanation of an amygdala hijack is simple. There is a lot more science involved – like the responses of the sympathetic and parasympathetic nervous systems. But for our purposes, this explanation is accurate even in its simplicity. The bottom line is that impact of an amygdala hijack creates physical havoc. The chemicals released as part of the hijack include ones that might help us react in the short term, but create high blood pressure, ulcers and can potentially impact our immune systems in the long run.

So a quick recap. We started at top left of the model at self-awareness. It is the foundation of emotional intelligence. It's about being aware of our emotions – the triggers that fire off emotional responses such as anger or fear. If I am aware of what sets me off (or what makes me deliriously happy for that matter) the more likely I am able to choose how I will respond. By the way, self-awareness is not about noticing the emotions of others – that comes later. This is about understanding what's going on inside of me and can require uncomfortable honesty.

Sports are driven by statistics – you need stats to be successful. Well, here are the stats for EI: self –awareness is the foundation for being able to manage emotions. Survey data shows if I am self-aware, I have a 50/50 chance at self-management. If I am NOT self-aware, the chances of my managing my actions drop to 4% or less. To say it differently, if I am not aware of my triggers, I have a 96% chance or higher of being a victim of my emotions.

Once we have experienced the power of emotions and understand how our responses work, we are ready for the second square, **Self-Management.**

Self-Management is about self-control – especially under pressure. It is the ability to be open to change and accept new ideas. It is also the capacity to persist despite obstacles and setbacks.

Let's look more closely at the idea of being open to change. Think of a time you were feeling challenged. It could have been when you and another school were trying to sign the same key recruit or another coach told you it was time to get off a shared field. What did you feel? Was the response something like, "Oh no, they're not! No one gets one over on me!" When you are feeling confronted, what emotions get invoked? You begin to see how self-awareness plays an important role. Self-management helps you *respond* rather than *react* to unexpected change.

Here's another example. Imagine you have an assistant coach who comes up with an idea for a practice routine that you don't like. What would be your response? Would it be to put them in their place and clearly spell out what will occur in practice instead? What we are looking for are any negative feelings that might get triggered - like disbelief, superiority or perhaps personal insult that someone on your staff would be so bold. If you are self-aware, you have the opportunity to recognize feelings and manage them before they take over. Just the awareness of a trigger may allow you to ask, "What do you have in mind?" Rather than blurting, "Are you kidding me?" And you never know when their creativity could create a win!

The next advantage of self-management is the ability to be persistent despite obstacles and setbacks. Think of a time you worked with a player who was stuck and didn't seem able to be learn new skills or improve his performance. Self-management is the ability that keeps you from being triggered and jumping down his throat. When you manage your reaction, you can be more open to the reasons he might be struggling. Or imagine you have a player like Tom who is incredibly talented; so talented he gets stuck in the pressure of being seen by pro scouts. He's so worried about looking good – or bad - that he loses focus during a game.

Let's look at their impact on you through the lens of the first two squares of the model. You've given them sound advice, having navigated young athletes through these problems before. However, your player is still making the same bush league mistakes. You begin to wonder if they'll ever understand as you feel the tension begin to move up the back of your neck. You realize you're triggered and are on the verge of getting angry. Good start. Self-management is your ability to choose to not let emotions be in charge. Rather, you take a deep breath and are able to look for other options.

We will go into the specific skills of self-management in the next chapter. What is important here is how self-awareness opens the door to self-management. If you recognize what's happening within you, you have the opportunity to find more ways to respond. Here are the stats: if you are aware, you have a 50/50 chance of self-managing. If you are unaware, the opportunity to give yourself other options drops to the neighborhood of 2% and typically no higher than 4%.

The gifts of self-management are increased self-control and a calm demeanor. You will find when you are competent in keeping your cool you will build trust in your organization. The people around you will work more effectively because they have confidence you won't fly off the handle without warning. Rushing to judgment represses creativity and limits the ability to see possibilities. When you are calm you can be more adaptable. You'll be able to see more options and take more creative, thoughtful risks. You can see obstacles as opportunities for growth rather than threats. Controlled emotions allow you to become resilient. You'll find you invest in the future rather than defend the past.

Let's move to the other side of the model, **Social Awareness**. This is where we find connection to others.

The definition of Social Awareness is being able to sense

others' feelings and perspectives. In a broad sense, it's the ability to read individuals and groups. It's the skill of understanding influencers, networks and group dynamics. How might that impact how you work with your team, administration or staff, your supporters and your fans?

Let's go back to the statistics as we build the picture of emotional Intelligence. If I am NOT self-aware, I can still be somewhat socially aware. We've learned from 25 years of data that my odds of success for being in tune with others if I am not self-aware can be up to 18%. In contrast, if I AM emotionally self-aware my odds of success double.

You can place your own value on being able to "read" the groups around you. Let's see how lack of social awareness blinded a coach to the needs of others and impact he was having.

> *Pete was certain he would prevail. After all, his track team always finished in the top three of the conference. All he needed to do was demand the gym and it was his. On this day, the volleyball team was occupying the space he wanted. Pete hadn't put in a facilities request, but why should he? He always took over the big gym this time of year. Pete was quite clear with the upstart new volleyball coach when he told her she had to leave. He made sure his tone conveyed his displeasure with her impertinence!*
>
> *You could have picked Pete's chin up off the gym floor when the A.D. came in to personally ask him to relocate his practice. The athletic director was clear when he informed Pete that the volleyball team was leaving at the end of the week for their conference tournament. Pete's only concern had been with his track team and hadn't even considered*

another team's priorities. He was rightly chastised and embarrassed at his own response.

The impact of being socially unaware has the potential of creating lots of problems including casting a shadow on a person's character. Pete was guilty of being thoughtless. However, he was seen by his boss and peer as being greedy, unreasonable and arrogant. Social awareness is about getting out of the cocoon of "it's all about me" to be able to see others and be empathetic. When we are able to understand others' perspectives, we can be open to ideas that are not ours and pave the way to collaboration.

Social awareness is also the ability to understand group politics, unspoken rules and dotted line control. For someone who is socially aware, it's easier to see the spoken and unspoken needs of the group. Consider what happens when that is not the case. The socially unaware are focused on themselves and blind to the needs of the group – like Ben or Pete, the track coach.

The final square in the model is **Relationship Management**. The emotionally intelligent coach holds a compelling vision that inspires others to follow. Because the coach is connected and aware, she (or he) finds the best with ways appeal to the group to create buy-in and community. She is able to provide the type of feedback that helps others learn and develop more quickly.

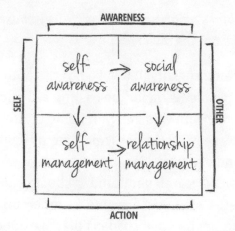

Bringing emotional stability allows a leader to create transformational change that feels safe rather than threatening. Communication becomes more effective because it can be crafted to match the needs of the audience. The skills of relationship management allow a leader to work through conflict with the least amount of damage. We call it delivering a hard message without being harsh. This type of emotional competence draws those around you into active commitment to a shared vision. And what more could a coach want in his or her organization?

Consider the value EI will bring to your organization. Your emotional intelligence will invite stability to your organization, which in turn will create an atmosphere that attracts learning, self-improvement and team commitment. As I tell my corporate clients, whatever you want to accomplish will occur more quickly and more effectively when you are an emotionally intelligent leader. In the next chapter, we will talk about the skills that will help you get there.

Practice Drills

Think of a time you've blown up at a game, practice or toward an athlete.

What was the trigger? (Or what triggered you?) I encourage you to dig into your memory to discover the 'story behind the story.' Maybe you were insulted or offended or threatened. Be honest with yourself...no one will check your work.

- What do you regret about blowing up?

- What could you have done differently to make the same point (if it was worth making)?

- If you hadn't blown up, what would have been possible?

Here is the next step in building the skill of self-awareness: Over the next week, keep a log of every time you feel emotions beginning to well up inside. Determine what triggered them and take note whether you managed the hijack or gave into it.

Consider these questions.

- What was the cause of the outburst?

- What was the cost?

- What was the benefit?

Note what you discover.

journal page

4

LEARNING EMOTIONAL INTELLIGENCE –
THE BEHAVIORS OF SUCCESS

"Out of control emotions make smart people stupid."

Daniel Goleman, 1998

In the last chapter, we talked about the emotional intelligence model and how each square related to one another. Now we can turn our attention to the behaviors of emotional intelligence and how can they be integrated into sports coaching. These are the first steps to create your EI competitive edge.

Emotional Intelligence is all about behaviors and the good news is that behaviors can be changed. A behavior is something we say or do. Behaviors – also called *competencies* - are recognizable, measurable and changeable. The *changeable* part is what's most important because it means emotional intelligence can be learned. Just as you change the position of your hand to improve your golf swing, you can change how you respond to emotional triggers.

Think of it this way – just because you did it last season does not mean you have to do it that way in the future. I will be teaching you to change in emotionally intelligent ways. That's why there are practice drills and journal pages at the end of every chapter. The more you practice EI behaviors, the more natural they will become.

I'll be honest - not all of these changes will be easy. You may be asked to challenge old behaviors. However, you'll learn new responses to replace the ones that no longer serve you. *Replacing* old habits with new ones is an important distinction because of the way the brain works. It's easier to create new neural pathways than to re-route old ones. So we'll focus on creating new habits, not fixing old ones. If you are up for it, I'll help you examine why you do what you do so you can discover more effective choices.

Let's review the value of emotional intelligence by the numbers. Remembering that success begins with self-awareness

- If you are self-aware, you have a 50-50 chance of demonstrating self-management. If you are not, the odds drop to 4% or less. That leaves you with virtually no chance of self-management.

- If you are self-aware, you double your likelihood of social awareness over someone who is not self-aware. The unaware person is more than 80% likely to misread a situation.

How do those statistics translate into value? The more you are aware of your emotions, the less likely you will be to fly off the handle and lose control. Unpredictable emotional outbursts from a leader create an air of mistrust and fear in the organization. When you are emotionally stable, people around you will become more confident in you and themselves. No one sets out to be an ineffective leader, but lack of self and social awareness can leave that impression – like Pete the coach who demanded the practice space and wasn't aware of his impact.

There is a more subtle but profound value to EI. Without self-awareness, we may think we are better (or worse) at managing situations than we really are. Remember the story of Ben. He was surrounded by discontent and if you recall, it was two years before they showed him the door. For all that time he held on to his misconceptions and assumptions despite the evidence before him. He was blind to all that was swirling around him. We can all be victims of the same blindness.

The truth is, we can only change those things we can see. So our practice drills will focus on translating self-awareness into behavioral changes.

Emotional intelligence is critical for you because your job as a coach is to deliver results through others. We will look at EI competencies that allow you

- Work more cooperatively
- Address and resolve conflict in healthy ways
- Motivate through influence (rather than just telling people what to do)
- Inspire individuals and groups
- Mentor and develop others

That covers most things a coach would want. So to begin the journey to emotional intelligence, we'll begin with a picture of the model to which we have added the competencies to each quadrant.

self-awareness	social awareness
• Emotional Self-Awareness	• Empathy • Organizational Attunement
self-management • Drive for Excellence • Flexibility • Emotional Self Control • Positive Perspective	relationship management • Conflict Management • Coach and Guide • Influence • Inspirational Leadership • Teamwork

Competencies are behaviors and since behaviors can be learned and changed let's see how that happens, one quadrant at a time. We'll build the skills of emotional intelligence in ways that work in sports.

The single competency in **Self-Awareness** is **Emotional Self-Awareness**.

self-awareness	
• Emotional Self-Awareness	

That's the ability to understand our emotions: where they come from and how they affect us. It's being able to recognize (and eventually anticipate) how we will react to events in our environment.

For example, how do you react when you are faced with a defiant student, an inept official or a sick child at home? What events are so volatile that they trigger an amygdala hijack? What's the impact of your emotional state on your performance or on the organization? Being emotionally self-aware is the ability to understand your triggers and recognize them as they occur.

Emotional self-awareness is also about being honest. It's the ability to look at your emotional responses objectively not needing to justify or judge yourself. Your willingness to acknowledge emotional reactions, receive feedback and gain insight into how people perceive you will be the basis for EI success. Emotional self-awareness is the ability to look inside and be honest about what you find. When you are self-aware, you are

- Mindful of your own feelings
- Honest with yourself about why those feelings occur
- Aware of the consequences of your emotions
- Aware of your strengths and limitations
- Willing to hear feedback

When you recognize that a sloppy official makes you angry, you've identified an emotional trigger. You'll find the more you can recognize triggers, the more you will be able to head off amygdala hijacks before they carry you away.

There are three ways to become more aware of your emotions and find areas for self-development. They are

- Understand yourself – examine your strengths, weaknesses and vulnerable areas.

- Ask others for feedback. This step takes courage. Begin by asking someone you trust to offer an honest assessment. Ask them what they see as your strengths and blind spots. Be open to what they have to share.

- Complete a formal assessment of your emotional intelligence. There are many good ones on the market. The one I offer is the Emotional Social Competencies Inventory by the Hay Group - the one endorsed by Daniel Goleman.

The good news is self-awareness can be developed. Begin by turning your attention inward to become aware of the emotions you feel. Be curious about when and why they begin.

Self-Management is the next quadrant of EI. It's made up of four competencies.

Drive for Excellence

This first competency is having a high standard for performance. When you drive for excellence you are willing to look for opportunities and take action on them – its being oriented toward achievement. The behaviors include looking for ways to improve, embracing new challenges and holding yourself accountable for your actions. Examples of driving for excellence are

- Honestly analyze situations and anticipate stumbling blocks

- Be willing to take reasonable risks

- Set measurable goals

- Commit to action rather than overanalyzing situations

- Be creative in finding answers – look in places that are not common or predictable.

Driving for excellence includes a willingness to learn, improve and change to meet and exceed your own standards.

> *Tim wasn't crazy about the idea, but the handwriting was on the wall. The NCAA was moving to adopt new specifications for baseball bats. California colleges had already adopted the new bats and were seeing changes in the game as a result of the new equipment.*

> *Rather than get caught up in the politics of the switch, Tim decided to make the best of it. He made a trip out to the West coast to learn all he could about new game strategies so he could get a jump on his competition.*

Flexibility

Flexibility is about adaptability and working effectively even while situations and people are changing. Coaches who are adaptable are willing to modify or change their ideas or perceptions based on new information or evidence.

Think of the story about Tim. In 2011, the NCAA issued new rules governing the type of bats allowed. The teams that were most successful immediately following the change were the ones that adapted their game to the ways the new bats responded. There were fewer home runs and effective "short games" became the winning strategies. Coaches who were high in flexibility didn't lose time fighting the change – they adjusted their approach and brought the new approaches to their teams.

Here are examples of being flexible

- Juggle multiple requirements easily

- Manage dynamic priorities and rapid changes easily

- Adapt plans to fit changes as they arise

- Remain flexible and calm under the pressure of change

- Adapt ideas and strategies based on new information or circumstances (like new specifications for bats)

Flexibility is choosing to be open and optimistic. It's *learned optimism* that enables you to respond positively to change. Unexpected change is inevitable, unfortunately it often triggers a negative reaction. That's natural because from the amygdala's viewpoint, change must be a threat because it often means losing something. So a negative default response is not surprising. Flexibility encourages you to see possibilities and adapt when others hesitate. It's a powerful competitive advantage!

Emotional Self Control

This competency is the ability to control impulsive emotions.

The fact is, we are human and emotions occur. The skill is in being able to apply the emotional brakes when your default is to lash out. Self control is being able to manage negative emotions that might be invoked in the face of provocation, hostility or escalating pressures. Successful behaviors are to

- Remain calm with stress is high

- Control impulses and display control

- Stay calm and positive, even when you are being emotionally triggered

- Stick to your work and not being overwhelmed with negative emotions

Emotional self control means controlling extremes of any emotion. It goes without saying that we should manage the negative emotions like anger and frustrations, but there is also a need to understand the limits of all emotions.

A coach shared the story of one afternoon when he was having such a good time laughing and joking with his staff that he inadvertently crossed the line and joined in a joke that had racial overtones - inappropriate for the head coach. He immediately recognized what he had done. He had been developing his emotional intelligence so instead of letting opportunity pass, he stopped the conversation and apologized for getting carried away. Emotional self control manages extremes of all kinds.

Positive Perspective

You've heard of seeing the world as a glass half full rather than half empty – that's having a positive perspective. It is a willingness to look for the good in situations and people. This offers a great opportunity to replace old behaviors with new.

The obvious job of a coach is to find out what's not working and fix it. Positive outlook gives you an alternative to the "find what's broken" standard coach mode and begin to see things differently. Looking through a positive lens means

- Seeing opportunities rather than threats

- Holding positive expectations

- Looking for what's working more than what needs to be fixed

- Believing the future will be even better than the past

- Finding the positive side or what can be learned in a difficult situation

One of the most powerful tools of the positive coach is *curiosity*. The meaning of curiosity is pretty simple – it is the desire to know. There is innocence to curiosity. Think of a small child who is fascinated watching a parade of ants. Theirs is curiosity with no judgment. Being curious is the opposite of making assumptions or jumping to conclusions.

Positive perspective will help you shift from looking for "blame" to finding "cause."

> *Tammy had been named head coach at the very end of summer. She was hired so late in the year that she was stepping into a locker room full of players she didn't know. She knew their history and understood that they would be nervous. According to the athletic director, her predecessor had been extremely controlling. In fact, one of the thicker notebooks she noticed on the shelf in her office was titled "Team Rules."*
>
> *When she walked in, the look on the players' faces ranged*

*from concern to outright fear. They saw her as the new
sheriff in town and didn't know if they would make the
grade, keep their scholarships or be thrown off the team.*

*As the new coach, Tammy realized she must to be
completely honest and inclusive with the athletes. So in
their first meeting she told them of her vision for the
program, how she saw great potential in the team and
what she would be asking of them. She didn't mince words.
Tammy told them she would demand their very best and in
return, said she would bring her A game- every day. She
finished by telling them she was a tough love coach. Then
she gave them a choice: buy in and stay or if it didn't sound
like what they had signed up for, step out with no penalties.*

Positive perspective for a leader says that if you can't change
the circumstances, find a healthy way to deal with them. In
Tammy's case, her positive, clear approach to a new team in a
new school translated into the best softball record in the
history of the school by the end of their first season together.

When multiple challenges seem overwhelming, holding a
positive outlook will help you remain focused and calm instead
of becoming overwhelmed by emotion or stress.

Drive for excellence, flexibility, emotional self control and
positive perspective round out the self-management
competencies. Let's move to the right side of the model to
introduce the competencies of working effectively with others.

Social Awareness is next. It is being able to recognize and
understand the emotions of others. The key to these
competencies is being able to get out of myself and connect
with others.

```
┌─────────────┬─────────────┐
│             │ social awareness │
│             │ • Empathy   │
│             │ • Organizational Attunement │
├─────────────┼─────────────┤
│             │             │
│             │             │
│             │             │
└─────────────┴─────────────┘
```

Empathy

Empathy is a critical EI skill because people generally don't tell you what they are feeling. So social awareness begins with the ability to pick up emotional cues. When you are empathetic, you can sense meanings behind what is said. You can pick up on partially or unexpressed thoughts and feelings. When you demonstrate empathy, you

- Tune into nonverbal cues to understand others' moods

- Listen deliberately (quieting the chatter in your head to be able to hear)

- Understand the viewpoints of others (even when they are different from your own)

- Understand why others make the choices they do (you don't have to agree to understand)

- Deal well with people of diverse backgrounds (*Diverse* means anyone who is different.)

One who is empathetic is open and curious – no preconceptions, no judgment.

Tyler came off the field in a rage. He had been pitching well until one ball got away from him. What should have been the final strike became a double that gave the other team the lead. He knew when the ball left his hand that it wasn't the pitch he wanted. He was so angry!

When he came off the field, he stormed to the far end of the dugout. It was clear he didn't want to talk to anyone. Kyle, the pitching coach, was good at sensing what others were experiencing and was skilled at responding at just the right time. He watched Tyler until the young man had a chance to calm down a bit and then quietly walked over to talk.

Organizational Attunement

Organization attunement is the ability to sense and understand relationship dynamics in a group. As a coach, you need to be able to identify those athletes with power over others as well as those who are susceptible to being influenced. It is also the ability to recognize the values and norms of the organization and how they affect the way people act. When you demonstrate organizational attunement, you

- Understand the politics in play
- Can read who has power and who can be influenced in a group
- Recognize emerging leaders as well as malcontents
- Understand the values and culture of the team
- Understand the informal processes within the team and how the players approach their work
- Know what is valued and what is not

Social awareness is critical in your line of work. There are so many elements of organizational dynamics at play and it only takes one person being out of sync to impact the entire organization.

> *Annie was finally a senior. She had been told she was a natural leader and had been waiting for the opportunity to show her stuff. It was early in their first semester and Annie was stepping up to what she thought was her rightful position as a leader.*
>
> *Dan had been watching team dynamics. New and returning players were working hard, but he sensed a negative undercurrent. So he began to watch more closely. One afternoon he was having the whole team take an extra lap for their lack of attention toward the end of practice. That's when he heard Annie tell the team, "Now you should all remember that you should never let up in practice or we'll all have to run extra laps." As the running continued, players began to separate themselves from Annie and Dan heard one freshman mutter, "bitch!"*
>
> *Coach Dan pulled Annie aside, to explain the difference between being a team leader and acting like their mother. He was able to combine empathy for Annie along with a lesson on organizational awareness. His aim was to help her be more aware of her impact so she could become a leader the team would be happy to follow.*

Once armed with the skills of social awareness, you are ready for the final stage of emotional intelligence. The potential of a high performance organization come together with **Relationship Management,** the ability to apply emotional understanding in dealing with others.

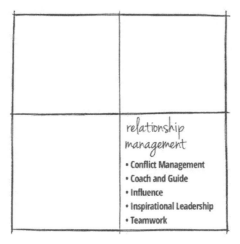

relationship
management
• Conflict Management
• Coach and Guide
• Influence
• Inspirational Leadership
• Teamwork

Effective working relationships within the team are critical. In fact, one basketball sportscaster observed, "You don't win with the best talent. You win with the five players who are able to play well together." But relationships can be unpredictable and must be actively monitored and managed. That's where the competencies of the last quadrant come in. The behaviors include conflict management, coach and guide, influence, inspirational leadership and teamwork. Let's look at them one at a time.

Conflict Management

This is more than just the ability to handle difficult individuals. It's being able to manage tense situations with diplomacy and tact. And it's being able to meet conflict face-to-face rather than avoid it. Healthy conflict management focuses on issues rather than the people. To successfully manage conflict you

- Bring disagreement and conflicts into the open

- Help de-escalate conflict

- Calmly communicate the various viewpoints to everyone concerned

- Focus on a larger goal valued by everyone

- Find a position that everyone can accept

Notice how conflict management relies on the competencies you've been developing – from emotional self control through organizational awareness. Your ability to manage conflict invites others to a place of emotional stability so differences can be resolved without inviting emotional hijacks.

Coach and Guide

This is the ability to enable (and encourage) long-term learning and development in others. If you are high in this competency, you help people develop themselves rather than always telling them what to do. This competency is broader than just teaching or training, the more traditional definition of coaching. If you're good at this, you will help people find their own ways to excel by providing feedback and encouragement. When you demonstrate coach and guiding competencies you

- Encourage others to be actively involved in their own development

- Offer specific, positive feedback

- Recognize and celebrate the strengths of the individual player and the team

- Encourage others to pursue their dreams, callings and passions

- Care about others' development

- Use accountability as a developmental tool

One key to helping others in their development is offering feedback. This isn't the type of feedback that begins with telling players what they did wrong. Feedback can be a delicate business because people can be sensitive. Emotionally intelligent feedback is constructive observation combined with *empathy* to offer positive reinforcement and encourage self-development. We'll talk more about feedback later and how to avoid the kind of negative feedback that triggers defensive reactions. You'll learn more about coach and guide in the next chapter.

Influence

Influence is the ability to have a positive impact on others. It involves persuading and encouraging others to get their support and buy-in. (In contrast with telling people what to do.) Influence is earning others' attention because they find value in what you offer. When you demonstrate influence, you

- Build agreement and support for ideas and approaches
- Enroll people by appealing to their self-interest
- Anticipate how others will respond to an idea and adapt your approach to fit
- Convince others by engaging them in discussion
- Work to build buy-in

You heard Tammy's story. She was the new head coach who stepped into the job at the very beginning of the school year. Tammy didn't rely on her position to win the hearts of her players; she offered a vision of a hopeful future and a picture of what it would take to get there. She used influence rather demands to win the hearts of her new team.

Inspirational Leadership

Inspirational leadership is assuming the role of visionary and leader. This is not about the formal position of authority but rather the behaviors of motivation and belief. People with this competency can effectively bring others together to accomplish mutual goals. They are able to build a strong sense of belonging within a team, leading others to feel they are a part of something bigger than themselves. When you demonstrate inspirational leadership you

- Inspire others by holding a vision or goal for the team

- Make the work engaging by keeping it connected to the vision for the future

- Motivate by creating a positive emotional environment

- Are proud of the team and let them know

- Lead by encouraging the team to always bring their very best

An inspirational leader is able to evaluate situations and understand what is needed. Inspirational leaders create high-performance work environments with lofty expectations and genuine praise.

Teamwork

Teamwork behaviors underscore how to work with others cooperatively. The competencies of teamwork focus on being a part of the *team* – not just as individuals who are playing as a group. Teamwork is about being competitive but not cutthroat. These competencies emphasize shared responsibility toward work and offering appropriate rewards for accomplishments. Teamwork is more than just a message – it requires work. Those high in teamwork will

- Create cooperative working relationships

- Build team identity and spirit
- Create a friendly, cooperative environment in the team (be on the lookout for bullying language, behavior or hazing)
- Ask for ideas and invite participation
- Reward appropriately and fairly
- Demonstrate and require respect

Creating a sense of teaming is fundamental for any team's success. And as you consider the practices of teamwork, it's good to recall all the teams you are a part of: your coaches, players, your organization and the community. You can practice teamwork in all of those places.

Now that you understand the behaviors of emotional intelligence, let's move to practicing them.

Practice Drills

Self-Awareness

Keep a journal of your feelings. This doesn't have to be a big production, but it will require that you take notes during the course of a day of your emotional triggers and responses. When you feel emotions invoked (delight, fear, anger – any emotion), write down what happened and how you responded. Be sure and capture any physical reaction (like tension in your neck, shoulders or stomach or racing heart).

Predict how you will react. Pick a challenging day you will face and anticipate situations you'll be in. It could be an all-department meeting that makes you feel anxious or watching an assistant coach at work that may invite frustration. Lunch with your staff may allow you to relax. Whatever the day holds, predict how you will react. Your job here is to practice recognizing and naming the feelings.   Later, notice the impact of being self-aware.

Self-Management

Make a list of the things at work that cause an impulsive emotional reaction for you. Think of situations when you "lose it." For example, "I get really angry when...."

Then, **create a game plan** for each of your examples that will allow you to prevent losing self-control. Focus on what would work for you. For example, "When I realize I'm getting angry, I can stop, breathe deeply, take a short walk and then go back to work."

Social Awareness

Pay attention to your interactions with other people for a day. Note how you act and react. Choose one or two interactions and ask yourself the following questions:

- What did I notice about their energy? Were they excited, angry, happy, frustrated, etc.?

- Did I listen to the person? Did I lose track of what they were saying because I was doing something else at the same time?

- Was I listening to them or to my own thoughts? Did I decide their motive without asking?

- Did I ask the other person questions about what they were saying?

- What did I notice about their feelings and emotions?

- Did I change my body language, facial expressions or tone of voice to help the other person feel comfortable, heard and understood?

Relationship Management

Assess where you are right now in each of the Relationship Management competencies. Note the areas where you would like to develop. Here's what to do:

- Next to each competency below, start by listing what you already do well

- Next, write down areas where you would like to improve

- Choose one or more competencies you'd like to work on – areas where you recognize a need or simply want to improve. Don't limit yourself to your athletic team. Look at the landscape of your life. You can choose your role of being the voice of your team in the community or the boss of an athletic staff or the one who manages parents, donors or alumni. Be curious and enjoy this exercise!

	EI Skills I have	What I want to develop	Where to try new behaviors
Conflict Management			
Coach and Guide			
Influence			
Inspirational Leadership			

journal page

5

TAKING NEW SKILLS TO WORK –
LISTENING AND QUESTIONING

"Tell me and I forget.
Teach me and I remember.
Involve me and I learn."
Benjamin Franklin

We introduced emotional intelligence to create the foundation for the new skills you'll be adding to your toolkit. As we delve further into ways for you to become more effective, we are going to draw from professional coaching – my kind of coaching - to enhance your sports coaching skills. As you may have noticed, it's time for us to invent a new term.

The linguistic challenge is that you're a coach – your job is to work in your sport and win games. I'm a coach – my job is to help people develop and grow through self-discovery. And as we talk about coaching – we use the same word but are not talking about the same skills. You teach, share knowledge of the game and help athletes improve their play. You correct what's not working in individual and team performance. On the other hand, I ask a lot of questions to help my clients become curious about their most pressing issues and help them find solutions within themselves.

We are both coaching. Same term – different meanings.

There are elements from my way of coaching that you will find helpful in sports coaching. You and I touched on some as we talked about the competency, *coach and mentor*. So as I teach you skills from my line of work, let's not stumble on the term *coach*. Instead, let's create and name a new role you can assume when you want a player to become more involved, creative and accountable for their development. We'll call it being a *conduit,* as in conduit coach.

A conduit is a natural path through which something is conveyed. As a conduit, you will help players see their own potential and find the way through their own ideas, initiative, accountability and responsibility. Think of conduit coaching as another set of skills – the skills of helping athletes fully participate in their own development.

The conduit coach takes an "ask" versus "tell" approach to developing others. When you put this hat on, you'll focus more on the athlete than the task. The conduit's job is not to "fix" anyone – you become then natural path to help them to correct themselves. The conduit leverages the accountability and responsibility created by the coachee (the athlete being coached) to effect change and create results. Here's an example –

> Aaron had the potential of being a great asset to the team
> and as a senior, had a lot to offer. The problem was his
> ability to follow the rules of the team. He was often just a
> little late to practice or a little lax in learning the new
> playbook. He was not upholding the standards of the team
> and Coach realized it was beginning to reflect in other

members of the team. They watched Aaron get away with little things and they all wanted to be exceptions, too. The staff had told Aaron more than once that there would be consequences if he didn't shape up. Nothing seemed to work. So finally, one day the coach called Aaron in after practice for a serious discussion but decided to take a conduit coaching approach.

"Son, we've been telling you for the past week that you need to tighten up on the team rules. And I'm curious, as you look back on your performance, what grade would you give yourself?"

Aaron, who was ready for another butt chewing, was NOT ready for that question. "I don't know what you mean."

The coach explained, "If you were on my side of the desk, watching a tight end named Aaron over the last week, what grade would you give him on team elements?"

"Well, I guess he could have done better..." Aaron stammered.

"That's what I think, too. This isn't the first time it's been mentioned. If you were in my place, what would you do?" Aaron didn't answer for a long time. Finally, the coach asked again, "What would you do?"

"I'd give me one more chance."

"And then what?"

"I'd throw my lazy ass off the team." Aaron looked quietly at the coach...he understood.

"Thanks, Aaron. Then that's what we'll do. See you

tomorrow."

When you are a conduit, you are nimble: able to respond when learning opportunities appear. Since you have gotten past old behaviors like getting angry or exploding, you can be present, curious and ready to create new ways for learning. And as in Aaron's story, you'll find ways to tap into your players' character as well as their physical abilities. Just an observation – in Aaron's story, the coach didn't relinquish his authority. If Aaron doesn't measure up, removing him from the team is still on the table.

The skills of a conduit we are going to introduce are

- Listening
- Asking powerful questions
- Giving responsibility and providing support
- Co-creating accountability

In this chapter, we will take an in-depth look at the conduit skills of listening and asking powerful questions.

Listening

Listening is part art and part science. You've heard of active and passive listening – that's a limited approach. Don't depend on those definitions as we talk about conduit listening. Active and passive listening assumes that listening is either being tuned in (aware) or not (hearing but not attentive).

Ours will be more robust than that approach. We will focus on different ways we listen. I'll describe three levels of awareness that are possible in listening and how we can be intentionally connected to what is going on around us.

Before we go there, let's begin by becoming mindful about listening. Our first step is to become aware of inhibitors to effective listening. First is the sheer pace of our world. Every coach I've worked with tries to squeeze as much as they can into a day. They work long hours and attempt to accomplish as much as possible, which often includes trying to do several things at once.

The technical description for this juggling act is "multi-tasking." The term was first introduced in the world of information technology in the 1970's. The truth is, though some machines can execute more than one task at a time, the human brain can't. Brain science (neurophysiology) has demonstrated that two thoughts cannot occur at the same time. Electronic pulses in the human brain occur sequentially. We can't physically listen to someone and do anything else at the same time.

This is all background as we turn our attention to how to listen. To set the stage for great listening, let's recall an experience that probably wasn't so great. Think of a time you were talking with someone and they were looking at their smartphone. Suddenly you realized they weren't listening to you. Their attention was on the screen. If you were feeling generous at the time, you might have given them the benefit of the doubt. If they were a repeat offender, you probably got angry. The truth is, even if they had the best intentions they were distracted by another brain process.

Here's what happens. When I'm bouncing between two tasks – like working at my computer and someone steps in and to ask a question - my brain stops working on the first task to quickly deal with the interrupt. Then I glance back to the screen and the process reverses. Then the question is asked and the process reverses again. Think of this process as start–stop-start-stop…you get the idea. The bottom line is, we may think we are multi-tasking, but in fact, we aren't doing either task effectively. Our brains don't effectively bounce between two tasks. Scott Peck, author and speaker tells us, "You cannot truly listen to anyone and do anything else at the same time."

What are the implications for the conduit coach? Again, think of the time you were talking with someone and realized they weren't really listening. What was the impact? Did you feel invisible? Unimportant? Being an adult in that situation, I might be able to say, "I'll come back when you have time." But, if you experienced this as a young person, you might feel stuck, helpless and not valued. Half listening has negative consequences. Listening is purposeful work that requires self-awareness and self-management.

We are going to examine three levels of listening available to the conduit coach. These "levels" describe where you put your attention. We'll show you how listening becomes an intentional skill.

Let's look at the three and how they impact your effectiveness as a conduit coach.

Level 1 - Internal Awareness/Listening

Level 1 describes our default mode. That's where my awareness is on myself. I may hear the words the other person is saying, but my attention is on how it applies to me. I am hearing my internal chatter more than what the speaker is saying.

To see how Level 1 works, read the next sentence. As you read it, be aware of the chatter in your head.

*The only thing standing between your team and a
championship is YOU.*

Notice how the chatter begins.

> "What does she know about us?"

> "Well, she's got us nailed!"

> "Is she forgetting about the rest of the team?"

> "What a stupid statement!"

It doesn't matter what the opinions are – just notice how loud
(and natural) the noise in your head is. That's the internal
chatter that gets in the way of giving our full attention to
others.

When I'm at Level 1 and another person is talking, I am often
judging what's being said by how it makes me feel. At Level 1, I
look for conclusions for myself. There is really only one
relevant question in Level 1 Awareness: What does it mean to
me? I may be nodding, saying "uh huh," but inside I'm having
another conversation. "When will he stop talking?" "What will I
say next?" "When is my next appointment?" "What will I do for
dinner?"

Let's give you an opportunity to experience Level 1. In your
next conversation, let your mind go anywhere it wants to
wander. If you are hearing about a wonderful meal, think of the
most wonderful meal you've ever had. If someone is telling you
a problem, let your mind go to the problems you are having or
how you would solve their problem. Don't stay with your
chatter for long - just take a moment, long enough to be aware
of it - then stop and check in to see how connected you are to
the other person. Are you really listening to them? Where is
your attention – with them or on your own thoughts?

Here are some key indicators that you operating at Level 1 Awareness:

- You are more concerned about how the situation applies to you than about the person talking

- You are making judgments about what is being said. (For example, "That's nonsense." "Why don't you take care of it yourself?" "I don't have time for this!")

To understand the impact of your listening at Level 1, go back to the time when you were talking to someone and felt they weren't really listening to you. How did it feel to be on the receiving end of partial or no attention? It's important to remember that it makes people feel unheard, devalued and unimportant. It's not the impact you want have on your assistants, staff or players.

Level 1 attention isn't bad. In fact, when I'm working with someone, I want them at Level 1 – investigating how our conversation impacts them. But as a coach, I can't afford for *me* to be there. One of the greatest (and least expensive) gifts we offer as coaches is our full attention. That's what we'll look at with the next two levels of listening.

Level 2 - Focused Awareness /Listening

At Level 2, I create a sharp focus on the other person and less on the outside world and myself. When I am at Level 2 Awareness, I quiet the chatter in my head so can I connect with the other person. The skill at this level is to listen beyond their words - to tune into their expressions, emotions and the energy they bring to what they are saying. I am so keyed in I get a sense of what is not being said. I am aware of what's really important.

When I'm focused, I can sense what energizes the other and what makes them withdraw. In fact, I am as aware of their energy as I am of their words. Empathy and curiosity are possible because I am not trying to decide my next move, what their issue might mean for me or what question I should pose next.

Here is a way to experiment with Level 2 listening. When you have your next conversation, quiet the chatter in your head and point your attention on the other person. If it seems challenging, don't worry, just keep working at it. This focused attention may be like exercising a new muscle. You are creating a new habit and it takes practice to self-manage internal dialogue. You'll want to practice keeping your attention on the other person, even if your inner voice wants to take over.

You'll discover there is power when you give your attention to another human. Recall a time when you felt someone really listened to you. Remember how they focused their full attention. What did you experience? What was the gift they gave along with their undivided attention? Now imagine the impact you will have when you take the time to listen at this level.

As a conduit coach, when your attention is at Level 2 you are focused on the other person and won't allow anything to interrupt you. When you are curious and fully engaged, you will discover the other person will open up.

Level 3 - Global Awareness/Listening

The deepest listening skill is Level 3. It is a focused awareness that takes in everything. Think of it as a combination of the spot light focus of Level 2 and at the same time being conscious of everything. It may be one of the most important skills of a successful coach.

I witnessed Level 3 in athletic coaching when I worked with a head softball coach. She had the ability to see the field of play as though she was looking at monitors in a production studio. Her awareness was so keen that she would see the dynamic between pitcher and batter as though it was on one screen while watching what was happening in the infield on another. Another mental monitor covered the outfield. She could take in all the action simultaneously with a soft focus of inclusion. Level 3 is a powerful combination of concentration and awareness.

There is something else you'll find with Level 3 awareness. When you connect at this level, you will be aware of the energy in the space. You can detect when and how it changes. You've probably heard athletes talking about being in their "zone." It's how they describe being at their best. They are calm, the pace of the game seems to slow down and they can take everything in with ease. That's a level 3 experience. Our job is to make sure you can find that zone of listening with ease.

If you are tempted to brush levels of awareness as more of that soft stuff, let's look at the science behind it. With the advent of magnetic resonance imaging (MRI), researchers have discovered amazing things about how the brain works. One of the most stunning discoveries in behavioral neuroscience is the identification of mirror neurons throughout the brain. Mirror neurons are like little sensing stations. They pick up signals from other people - sensing others' emotions. They allow us to navigate effectively through human relationships. These mirror neurons allow us to consciously (or unconsciously) detect someone else's emotions. Mirror Neurons provide the scientific foundation for what we are calling Level 3 awareness.

You have probably experienced your mirror neurons at work. Think of the time when you walked into a room and you got a "sense" that something was wrong – there had been a fight or there was great sadness – or some other strong emotion. And you sensed it even without a word being spoken – an example of an innate ability that can be practiced and improved.

Your mirror neurons are translating emotional energy from others to you all the time – it's a matter of quieting the noise of Level 1 to engage, receive and translate the transmissions.

Think of the implications - with practice, you will be able to detect sadness, lightness and shifts in attitude. You can become conscious of the underlying mood, tone or impact of a conversation. The more you practice the skills of Level 3 awareness, the more you will become attuned to an environment full of information. The reverse is also true – by that I mean, you can intentionally set the tone in a group. Just as you pick up on the energy of others, they respond to you. Your emotions and actions can prompt followers to mirror your feelings and intentions. Think of the potential. As an astute coach you can work to shift the energy in a halftime locker room by channeling determination and hope to your team.

We are wired for emotional connection. Our teams are wired to respond. The competency is available to you. Practice is what will make it real.

As you think about practicing a heightened sense of awareness, know that Level 3 includes everything you can observe with your senses; what you see, hear, smell, and feel, the tactile as well as the emotional sensations. Level 3 includes action, inaction, and interaction. One of the benefits of learning to listen at Level 3 is you also have greater access to your intuition. Your intuition allows you to receive information that is not directly observable. At Level 3, your intuition will be highly engaged as you read the energy, mood and attitude of the person/people with whom you are talking. With practice, you will be able to pick up on everything else in the space. You will be able to take advantage of what you sense in a room.

When you become adept at turning down the voice in your head and dialing up all other available information, you will be engaging one of the most powerful tools of a conduit coach.

Look around, most people listen at Level 1. Your new ability to listen deeply will invite trust and give people a sense of being valued. It will set you apart and is another competitive advantage in the game of working with people.

Let's move to the next important skill, powerful questions.

Powerful Questions

There are questions and then there are questions. We'll look at several types to understand where they are most effective. Our focus will be on conduit questions – those aimed at helping the player find answers for themselves. In professional coaching we refer to these as powerful questions.

A powerful question is one that invites the recipient to look deeply to find an answer. To become adept at these, you'll want to understand the nature and other types of questions that are available - then we'll practice constructing powerful questions.

First, there are three broad categories of questions: closed, open and leading.

A **closed-ended** question is one that can typically be answered by a simple "yes" or "no." The questioner is looking for a very narrow bit of information. Closed-ended questions can be used for clarifying facts, verifying information already given or controlling a conversation. All are credible goals for a sports coach who is questioning for performance, clarification or results. Closed-ended questions can be a valuable tool. The problem occurs when they are the only type of question used. Here are some examples of closed questions

- Did you do it?
- Was that a good idea?
- Would you choose that play again?

These questions don't invite dialogue or creativity, only data.

The easiest way to recognize closed question are to know the words that typically begin closed questions: is, are, do, did, does; would, should, could; was, were and have.

The impact of a closed-ended question is to limit conversation.

The second type, an **open-ended** question is designed to encourage thought. It invites a full, meaningful answer drawn from the knowledge and/or feelings of the person being asked. Open-ended questions are typically objective. They ask about the future and possibilities.

- What were your choices?
- How would you evaluate your impact?
- What would you choose next time?

Open questions are sometimes referred to as journalist questions because they typically begin with the words *who, what, when where, why* and *how.* These questions are designed to get the other person talking and looking into their own experience for answers.

The third category is **leading questions**. A leading question is one in which the person asking wants a specific answer. The leading question is worded to prompt the respondent to answer in a particular way. We've all heard attorneys in TV dramas ask questions like, "Is it true that you tried to slip that package into the defendant's briefcase without their knowledge?" or "What were you thinking while you were embezzling the payroll?"

Leading questions are used when the questioner believes he already knows the answer or how to solve the problem. He is simply gathering data to reinforce what he has already decided.

Leading questions won't be particularly helpful in your role of conduit coach. They are full of assumptions and judgment and can be a sure fire way to undermine trust.

Granted, part of your job is to solve problems. However, the other part is to be a conduit who allows others to grow by helping them find their own solutions. Here's what happens when a coach chooses to enable a player's learning rather than giving him an answer.

> *Jim had been through this a thousand times as a coach. A young player gets so wrapped up in the fury of the game, they lose control and play erratically. Sometimes they try to be a hero – forgetting everything they've learned about being on a team in an attempt to win points. Typically, the harder an athlete tries to fix a broken play or be a "star," the more things go wrong.*

Devonte fell into that category. He was a great runner and had potential, but he couldn't seem to manage himself—even in a simple scrimmage. He was always ready to showboat or pull tricks to get the ball. He wasn't learning the system and created distractions for the rest of the team.

It was time for the coach to intervene, so he pulled Devonte aside. The team occasionally used a sports psychologist who offered a couple of different "get yourself under control" exercises. Coach thought he would just assign one of them to his unpredictable running back.

Before jumping in with orders, Coach stopped himself and asked a question instead. "Son, I noticed when the pressure's on, you don't stick with the game plan. What's going on?"

Devonte considered the question and said, "When things aren't going good, I want to make sure we make a play."

Coach stopped himself before he jumped into a lecture about who's in charge and asked, "What happens when you do something unexpected?"

"Well, sometimes I make a great play!"

"And when you don't, what's the cost?"

Devonte looked blank, so Coach asked again, "What's the impact on the rest of the team?"

The young man coughed uncomfortably and said, "They don't know what I'm doing or how to help me."

"This isn't sandlot football. We're practicing so we run from the same playbook. When you think about this team,

what will make you a more valuable player?"

At that point, Devonte realized where the coach was pointing. He was being asked how he could act more responsibly as a player. That's when the conversation about maturity and responsibility began.

After a few minutes their talk ended with Coach asking, "What will you do differently?" Devonte said he intended to study the playbook more and watch the fullback who was a great team player. And he would try one of the breathing exercises the team had learned from the sports psych guys to settle down and manage his "team of one" impulses.

There is no doubt the coach could have invested less time – maybe as much as 5 minutes – by telling Devonte what to do. The advantage of this approach was the young athlete had to examine his behavior in relationship to the team. Devonte had to provide the answers and they were his answers not the coach's.

When people discover answers for themselves and say them out loud, there is a sense of ownership that doesn't come when they are told what to do. Ownership is the first step toward accepting responsibility and becoming personally accountable.

Another key differences between a coach who is solving problems and one focused on being a conduit is the purpose of questions. If you are working to solve a problem, your questions will be focused on the data surrounding the issue. If you want to help an athlete find their own solution, your questions will focus on the person rather than the problem. That allows your player to find his own answers. To make the distinction between the types of questions easier, here are samples -

Questions that gather data and solve problems

- What's the problem?

- What's the root cause?

- Have you done anything about it?

- Why isn't it fixed yet?

- How will you keep this from happening again?

Questions that provide a conduit for someone to find his or her own answers

- What do you want to work on?

- What is working? What is not working?

- How do you want the situation to be?

- What do you need to do to see a change?

- What is one action you could take to ensure success?

- What insights are you gaining?

Try reading the two sets of questions out loud and notice the difference in intent, energy and impact.

The second set creates a conduit for self-diagnosis and discovery. Since both types of questions are available, it would be helpful to recognize which style is your default. The way to discover that is to listen to the questions you ask.

If you discover that you typically go into problem solving so you can fix what's broken, you may want to expand your range and practice being a conduit part of the time – as Jim did. The more you practice conduit coaching questions, the more your athletes will own the responsibility for their development. As was the case with Devonte, most people accept and often welcome the opportunity to be in control of their own future.

Let's pause and be clear. I'm not saying that one set of questions is good and the other, bad. Both types of questions have value. What's important is that you recognize the difference. I want you to have options that allow you to choose the best approach based on what you see in the moment - conduit for development or problem solver.

The next element of asking questions is to examine the impact of the words you choose. We will look at three words that start many of our questions: *what, how* and *why*. These three words begin most open-ended questions. When you understand their meaning and how they are perceived, they become more meaningful choices. Here are the distinctions -

> **What** asks to the future and points to possibilities. It is an excellent question to ask early in a conversation because it ignites creativity. "What" starts some of the best conduit coach questions.
>
> > "What do you think?"
> >
> > "What have you considered?"
> >
> > "What is your diagnosis for your hitting challenges?"
>
> **How** begins to narrow a conversation. Asking how something is done stops gathering ideas and points the conversation toward a single idea or solution. When you ask, "How would you do that?" you have now limited the

conversation to a single idea. *How* is a valuable question, just don't ask it until later in a conversation after there has been time for exploration.

Why looks to the past and is a forensic question. When we ask about the past it's often to explain or justify behavior. Be cautious with your use of "why" because it is often heard as accusatory or judgmental. Unless you need history, don't overuse it. Think of *why* as salt. A little bit can brighten a dish of food. Too much can have a negative impact. "Why" is a question for a conduit coach to avoid.

Just as the words you choose have meaning, so does your intention. When I was new to sales, I had a manager who would ask, "Help me understand why you choose that." It didn't take long before I only had to hear the first three words to know I was in trouble. The words said "help me understand..." but the energy said, "what were you thinking???"

The energy and attitude behind your questions count. Don't try to ask conduit coaching questions when you are anxious, angry or trying to solve a problem. People will notice the difference immediately. I still cringe when I hear the words, "help me understand..."

The length of your questions also has impact. When you use too many words, you begin to point to the answer you think they should find...that's how leading questions are created. Instead, try a powerful question.

The professional coaching term *powerful question* means open-ended and short – really short. A good rule of thumb is seven words or fewer. The beauty of short questions is there are no wrong answers and they open the space for exploration – for looking in every corner of the consciousness. Here are some examples.

- What do you want?

- What's the value?

- What's the cost?

- What do you know?

- What do you experience?

Open-ended questions evoke clarity, discovery, insight, action and commitment – powerful *short* questions add punch.

The last conduit skill that blends listening and questioning is the self-management skill of waiting. I wish I had a fancier term to describe it - this is the discipline of asking a question and then stopping to allow the other person to answer. Many new coaches (I'm talking about my type of coach here) do what we call question stacking. They'll ask one question – and if there isn't an immediate response, add another. Still no answer? They'll ask their question a third time in a slightly different way. It never works well because while the coachee is working on the first question, the coach is down the road to the third question and the conversation is out of sync.

When you ask a question, ask just one and then welcome the silence that follows. The person is thinking – carefully considering what you've just asked. You can be confident, especially if you've asked a powerful question with punch, that they're thinking hard. You'll be able to see it in their eyes. It is a perfect time for you to practice Level 2 awareness.

As you give your coachee time, don't be concerned about the silence – it's your friend. If you wonder how long is long enough, try the 7-second rule. You ask one question and then be quiet for seven seconds. All sorts of good results can occur in as little as seven seconds. That's where the discipline comes in because even 7 seconds can feel like an eternity when you are just beginning to build the skill.

We've covered listening, questions, language and intention. Now it's time to practice.

Practice Drills

Listening

Levels of Awareness/Listening: Since there are three levels, the place to start is to experience shifting among the three levels. Find a situation where you are a listener and intentionally shift from one level to another. It's good to look for a time when you are not in charge and not responsible for the outcome. Look for a place like a church service, restaurant or presentation when you're in the audience.

1. Begin by allowing the chatter in your mind to occur. Instead of becoming embroiled in it, just notice it and the different directions it can go if you allow it.

2. Now, shift your focus to the person talking. Intentionally quiet the chatter. Be curious about what they are saying and their energy. If the chatter tries to interrupt you, don't let it. Stay focused on the other person.

3. Finally, practice the "soft focus" of Level 3. There are three parts to the practice:

    -   Keep the internal chatter under control.

    -   Focus on the other person.

    -   Allow yourself to focus broadly on your environment – the people in the room, temperature, ambient noise, whatever is in the space. Don't get lost in any of the elements (like wondering why the air conditioning is so cold) – that would be about you and takes you to Level 1.

If you slip and find yourself at Level 1, it's okay,
just shift back to take it all in once more.

The last step of this practice is to take notes about on what you
experienced when you were shifting your attention –

- Was it hard? Was it easy?

- What did you do that worked or helped you regain
control if your attention strayed?

- Where else can you practice this skill that would help
you as a coach?

Powerful Questions

Open-ended, closed and leading questions – becoming self-
aware

Your first practice is to understand habits and default
behaviors. Take a notebook with you over the next two days
and make note of your questions - the questions that you hear
in your head and the ones you ask out loud. Feel free to use
your own shorthand, but keep track of the three categories –
open, closed and leading questions. At the end of two days,
notice where you spend most of your time.

Open-ended, closed and leading questions – self-
management

Once you begin to understand your defaults you're ready to
introduce some changes. We'll begin with a practice of open-
ended questions.

- Take the list of words that begin open-ended questions
(*who, what, when, where, how* – we are intentionally
leaving out "why") and practice creating questions that

begin with those words. You can practice anywhere – at home, in your office, when you're on the phone. Listen to your questions and if you hear closed or leading questions begin, simply stop and reformat them as open-ended questions. ("Why did you do it that way?" can become "What were your choices?") You will be pairing self-awareness with self-management.

- If you find you're already good at open-ended questions – or if you're ready to move to the next step of practice, start making those questions short and powerful. Remember the rule of thumb is seven words or less.

- Now add the skill of silence. Ask one question – just one – and allow the other person the silence to think, discover and then answer.

- Finally, notice the impact these practices have on you. As you begin to become fluent in conduit skills, notice the impact you are having on those around you.

journal page

6

THE JOURNEY: WHAT TO TAKE WITH YOU WHAT TO LEAVE BEHIND

"Curiosity is more important than knowledge."

Albert Einstein

On your journey to becoming a conduit coach, let's shine a spotlight on three habits. I'll encourage you to take one with you and leave the other two behind.

The first habit is **curiosity**. Curiosity is a conduit competency to be embraced and nurtured. The other two, **assumptions** and **judgment** are barriers that should be recognized (realized, perhaps) so you can leave them behind.

Let's begin with curiosity. Albert Einstein gave a lot of credit for his success to curiosity when he observed, "I have no particular talents – I am only passionately curious."

Curiosity is the energy that fuels the desire for more information. It is the eagerness to learn or know. Think of curiosity as the art of being inquisitive. Remember when I talked about the simplicity and intensity of a small child watching a parade of ants? That's a perfect example of curiosity with no preconceptions. A youngster will focus on what those ants are up to and where they are going – not concerned with why. That's the artful level of curiosity we are talking about.

There is a competitive advantage to being curious and it is twofold. Curiosity invites new information to be discovered. Think about it. When I'm certain of the answer, I don't even look at other options! When curiosity (rather than certainty) becomes your default, you'll find yourself and those around you more willing to play with whatever shows up.

Here is where we are headed that may be new. Consider - you were hired as a coach because of your knowledge of your sport. You are paid to know how to fix problems, recruit talent and win games. You were hired for your expertise. That's a lot of certainty - which is not a bad thing, but it can be seductive. Being an expert can become an unexamined comfort zone. It's the comfort zone of thinking you know the answer to questions automatically. In that frame of mind, you may forget to be curious.

Certainty may feel comfortable (and safe), but can lead to *knowledge atrophy*. That's what happens when the world changes and the coach doesn't. Remember the story of the baseball coach when the NCAA changed the composition of bats. He was ahead of the pack in developing a new winning approach as a direct result of his curiosity. It opened the door to engage new strategies before they were being presented as a clinic at a national conference. That's what I mean by competitive advantage. Curiosity opens the door to be a trendsetter rather than a trend follower.

The gift of curiosity will draw your attention in different directions – instead of the one path called "looking for the answer." The curious conduit coach relies on questions and more questions in order to learn. Let's look at one way curiosity salvaged a relationship and changed everything.

Kayla played second base. Her coach was working to balance his athletic coaching with being a conduit. One afternoon during practice, it was obvious that Kayla didn't have her head in the game. She was disengaged, easily distracted – really doing a lousy job. Coach called to her a couple of times to focus, work through her sluggishness – things like that. An hour into defensive work he was disgusted with Kayla's performance and showed it.

Greg had coached long enough that he knew what was happening. The team was still in pre-season and it was the time when players had a hard time staying mentally engaged. Typically one reminder brought a good player back into focus, but it wasn't working with Kayla. The more frustrated Coach became, the more resistant Kayla became. He was ready to read her the riot act. That's when he remembered what he had learned about emotional intelligence from his executive coach, "It doesn't hurt to be curious and ask a question or two first. You always have the option of telling afterwards."

At a break in practice, Coach walked up to Kayla as she was glancing at her smartphone. There was another infraction – no phones on the practice field, no exceptions! Instead of blasting her, he took a deep breath to calm himself and asked what was going on. Then he stood back and waited for the expected excuses: classes are hard, I was up all night writing a paper, I had a fight with my roommate – he had heard it all before.

Kayla's shoulders slumped and Coach noticed she was pale. She told him that just before she stepped onto the field she had gotten word that her mother was sick and had been taken to the hospital. Her dad told her there wasn't anything she could do, but she was really worried. Then she apologized for her practice.

Coach was floored. First he was embarrassed because he had been ready to give her a piece of his mind. Even when he chose to ask a question instead of chewing her out, he assumed she would have some trite excuse. He was ready with a sharp response. Greg was grateful for all the things he hadn't said!

When Kayla told him what was going on, he felt an immediate shift into conduit mode. "What would you like to do?" he asked.

"I'd like to stay and practice. My dad said he would call as soon as he knew something and for me not to worry. I need to keep busy and would like to stay." He patted her on the shoulder and said, "Keep your phone with you. If you need to leave early just give me a wave then grab your gear and go."

Kayla had a much better second half of practice and when she packed up to leave, she waved a "thanks" in Coach's direction. He stood, watching her go, thankful that he had asked that question. Choosing curiosity over judgment kept him from doing something he would have regretted!

We all have a tendency to look for answers. It's part of our make up. When there's a problem, there must be a fix. Like, why is the defensive end dropping his shoulder? Why won't the tennis player charge the net? Why won't his 3-point shots drop in?

Questioning is a necessary and important part of the job. However, as we learned in the previous chapter if we only ask questions to diagnose problems, we can create the trap of assuming every situation is a problem. When we are in problem solving mode, our default is to look for what's wrong. After all, problems need to be fixed. The assumption is either something or someone is broken. Notice how the energy of brokenness begins to feel like a downward spiral.

Curiosity is the anecdote and if you are going to harness its power, there are a few things that need to be unlearned. First there are the years of training that problem solving is the only (or most valuable) approach to athletic coaching.

By the way, I don't mean to single coaches out in these examples. We, humans, learn the lessons of problem solving everywhere. Think of how the formal education system works. From our earliest years, we're trained to gather information by asking specific questions to help determine the correct answer. And because the measure of success in school is passing the tests (determining right from wrong) - we learned to search for the "right" answers – and generally there was only one. As part of the journey through the educational system, we learned that questions were used to narrow possibilities and finally zero in on the solution. Albert Einstein said, "It is a miracle that curiosity survives formal education."

The process of deductive reasoning doesn't invite exploration and over time can blind us to other possibilities. Consider your experience as a coach. How many solutions might be possible for any given situation? And if your situation really has only one solution, how many different paths might get you there? A conundrum occurs if the approach I use to develop a great offensive player isn't working with the kid standing in front of me. Curiosity is the answer.

The gift of curiosity is about discovering paths we might not otherwise imagine. Curiosity invites new information and collaboration. It is an ideal tool for a conduit coach because your purpose is to enroll the athlete to join you in finding options.

When it comes to a player's development, the athletic coach may know a lot about the game and what generally works with people, but it is the athlete who knows himself and how to make the advice and instruction work.

Look at golfer Jim Furyk. He has the most unconventional swing on the tour - one that no golf pro would teach and that most would try to correct. One commentator said it looked like Furyk was trying to swing inside a phone booth. Conventional wisdom might have told a young Jim Furyk to clean up his swing. Fortunately, that didn't happen – or he ignored it. Furyk knows his capabilities and what works for him and at the time of this writing was ranked fifth on the PGA tour, having earned $4.5 million for the year. Imagine what is possible if we just let go of "knowing."

Making assumptions isn't confined to the coach. Sometimes players make their own assumptions.

> *Craig played outfield but his real talent was hitting. The challenge was his on-again-off-again concentration. He worked hard to do what the coaches asked but there were times when he was too casual – almost lackadaisical on defense. So the coach called me in hopes of finding a way to help him.*

In our first conversation, Craig echoed the same frustration the head coach had mentioned – he got too relaxed, even disconnected, from the game when he was playing defense.

He kept repeating he was having problems keeping his head in the game so I asked Craig to tell me more about that. The look on his face was pained. "Coach brought in a motivational speaker. The guy told us that to really control our game we needed a routine of relaxation and breathing – emptying our heads of all other thoughts. He said we should focus on relaxing. The coaches keep telling me that when I have a trouble concentrating, that's what I should do. So I try. The problem is, it doesn't work for me!"

"What about it doesn't work?"

"I'm a pretty relaxed guy. I've never had a problem getting too wound up in the game. I kind of go the other way. So when they tell me I have to take a deep breath and empty my head, I lose my concentration."

I had no idea where our conversation would go next when I asked, "Okay, describe how you are when you are playing at your best."

"I'm loose, watching the game and ready to jump if the ball comes my way. If I try to do what that motivational guy suggested, I get too distracted and relaxed."

"Craig, our job to find the best method for you to be at your best. If you were to tell yourself the right approach for you, what would it be?"

He was quick to reply, "I'd tell me, 'you're not like those other guys. Don't do all that mind-relaxation stuff.'"

"Good idea!" I told him. "Your job is to go out and mentally prepare the way that works for you and see what happens."

Craig assumed that advice that works for 90% of young athletes would work for him. But it didn't

It was curiosity that led to the questions. If we hadn't looked for what was right for him, he might still be stuck in someone else's answer. I didn't know exactly what he should do, but he did. Craig was right in his assessment. He became an all-conference outfielder with a batting average of .371 and the conference leader in stolen bases. He played loose and ready...in his own way.

To practice curiosity, you can begin by building the habit of asking questions first. And remember to do it with simple childlike curiosity.

Craig's story also points us to the second major idea we want to cover here – the problem with making assumptions. An assumption is a story we make up to fill in for something we don't know. The dictionary definition is "a thing that is accepted as true or as certain to happen, without proof."

If you are like me, you make assumptions all the time. It comes from our universal struggle to understand. We make assumptions to fill in details, paint the rest of a picture – to create clarity for ourselves. The problem is that assumptions are fiction. They are based on our values and beliefs, not the other person's. After all, we can't see into someone else's mind. We can't really know what causes a person to make a choice without asking him.

The risk in making assumptions – making up a back-story for someone else's actions — is that our assumptions then affect the way we perceive the person and the situation. It's why the coach initially perceived Kayla, the softball player, as a slacker. That was his assumption – the certainty he created. What's scary about assumptions is we begin to believe they are true. That's when we lose the motivation to find out what is really going on.

In the book, *The Four Agreements*, the author Don Miguel Ruiz describes the challenge of making assumptions.

> *"The problem with making assumptions is that we believe they are the truth! We invent a whole story that's only truth for us, but we believe it. One assumption leads to another assumption; we jump to conclusions, and we take our story very personally. Making assumptions and taking them personally creates a lot of emotional poison, and this creates a whole big drama for nothing. We make assumptions, we believe we are right about our assumptions, and then we defend our assumptions and try to make someone else wrong. We even assume we are right about something to the point that we will destroy relationships in order to defend our position."*

Assumptions are sneaky. We can be in their grasp before we realize it. Here's a signpost to help you recognize when you are in the land of assumptions - so you can get out as quickly as possible. The signpost is also the third habit we want to examine – rushing to judgment.

Have you noticed how much judgment you hear in the chatter that assumptions create in your head? By the way, I'm not talking about the kind of judgment you use when you are evaluating talent. The type of judgment we are talking about here doesn't engage wisdom or discernment. It's the process of jumping to conclusions without supporting information. When we make assumptions, the next step is to rush to judgment. And even if there isn't malicious intent, there are typically negative repercussions. Judgment is a habit that we learn to rely on because it's easy and seems to provide clarity. It also provides the comfort of *knowing* even though it's a false knowing. Sadly, it takes almost no time to create snap judgments.

What's the cost? That will be yours to discover in your situation. If you are really curious, begin by becoming keenly aware of the power and frequency of your assumptions. You'll find judgments are also sneaky. Not only do they piggyback on assumptions, but they too pose as truth.

At this point in our journey, the question becomes how do we begin to eliminate assumptions and judgment. We start by focusing on what is possible in a situation rather than what's missing. The shift is from fixing a problem to looking for possibilities.

The first step is to begin to rush to curiosity rather than judgment. Go back to the lessons of emotional intelligence. Become aware of triggers that invite you to create stories and judge others. Kayla's coach believed he had heard all the excuses for a bad practice. He had initially been triggered and his anger invited him to create a reality that wasn't true. The good news is he resisted the story he made up and chose to pause and ask questions rather than depend on his assumptions. And he learned the truth. When we understand our triggers, we can stop the fantasy and rely on curiosity and questions.

Here is a tip - the opposite of judgment and assumptions is

curiosity. When you realize you are headed down the wrong path, it's easy to shift. As you look around and begin to ask questions rather than create assumptions, I bet you'll find great reasons to leave assumptions behind. Even though creating a story may seem faster at the time, like Greg, Kayla's coach, you'll save energy and churn by operating from a foundation of facts. It's time for some practice.

Practice Drills

Leaving assumptions and judgment behind

Since you've practiced self-awareness, use your heightened
attention to notice the assumptions that show up in the course
of a day. Tune into the voice of 'explanations' in your head and
recognize the explanations are typically assumptions. Here are
just a few places to look

- A driver cuts you off in traffic and you decide why they
  are rude (a rich guy in a Porsche, a sloppy worker in a
  pickup truck, a ditz driving a mini-van...you get the
  drift).

- You get a note from an administrator that some NCAA
  rules are changing.

- A student texts you to say they are going to be late.

There are countless opportunities. In this practice you don't
need to do anything but notice. However, if you want to go to
the next step, also notice how detailed the stories and
assumptions can become. By the way, resist the temptation to
judge others when they make assumptions. Realize that's just
another way to judge. ("I make up a few stories, but Sara really
gets carried away.") The truth is, we don't know what others
are thinking. And if we think we do, it's an assumption.

Taking curiosity with you

Once you have discovered when and how your assumptions
begin and take root, choose to be curious instead.

- Curiosity's first job is to replace the story with questions. "I wonder…" or "I am curious about…" are good places to start.

- The second thing is to notice the shift in energy that occurs when you choose curiosity over certainty. It may take a little practice, but be aware of the energy of each. Judgment is often a heavy feeling. Curiosity is light. If our energy is finite, where do you want to invest yours?

journal page

7

CREATING ACCOUNTABILITY,
SHARING REPONSIBILITY

If it is important to you, you will find a way.
If not, you will find an excuse.

Think of creating accountability and sharing responsibility with your athlete as the pot of gold at the end of the conduit coaching rainbow. You'll know when accountability is working its magic when you see the light in a player's eyes that says they've found something in themselves they want to improve.

The conduit view of accountability is an alternative to the more traditional approach of telling athletes what to do. Rather than starting with instructions, help your player discover where he should focus his efforts through your skills of conduit questioning and listening. Then you can guide him to create his own accountability. Often you won't even need to provide instructions unless it's a brand new skill. Self-realization often ignites the motivation to change. You'll love the energy that accompanies a light-bulb look of discovery, excitement and determination. Rather than explain how it works, let me share a story.

Rick, the pitching coach, was frustrated. It was the beginning of the season and it seemed as though his three best pitchers forgot everything they had practiced in pre-season once the real games began. What was even more frustrating was they exhibited three different versions of incompetence on the mound. One was too tenuous – afraid to be aggressive. The second was far too sure of herself – she would shrug off Rick's suggestions – believing she really didn't need to change. She often fell back into old habits that didn't work. The third pitcher would get mad when things didn't go right on the mound and blame everyone but herself. Her favorite trick was to refuse to look at the catcher or Rick when things began to go bad. The lack of results from the three was pointing to a disastrous season.

At the end of every game, Rick had done what pitching coaches do. He had gone through the films, edited and added comments, created individual practice routines and given the package to each of the pitchers. Only nothing changed. It wasn't like the three players didn't know the drill. They worked through the practice plans Rick gave them yet when they stepped onto the mound for a game it was as though they had learned nothing. Rick was at his wit's end!

That's when the head coach walked by his office and said, "I noticed you've had better days, what's going on?"

Rick laid it all out – the three very different problems, the amount of work he was putting in and the lack of progress he was making. His boss empathized and then asked, "If you were going to try something radically different, what would it be?" Rick was so frustrated that he threw up his hands and said, "I'd give them the raw footage of their game day pitching, have them analyze themselves and create their own practice routines."

"Great idea."

Rick took a deep breath – the idea felt a little scary – trying something so different. But he had tried everything he knew. So that's what he did. He called the pitchers in and let them know that he would be asking them to be responsible for discovering and overcoming their own barriers. He gave them their films and assignment to self-diagnose and design workouts. He told them that if they had problems or questions to come to him.

One pitcher responded immediately. She worked through her films and came back the next day with some great insights. She was amazed by what she learned by watching herself with a critical eye. She showed Rick what she planned to work on and he agreed. Armed with new insight and determination, she headed out to the bullpen.

The other two pitchers had been caught off guard by the assignment and showed up the next day empty-handed. They were used to being told what to do and didn't know how to respond to this new request - so they did nothing. With the success of the first pitcher under his belt, Rick held to his plan. He insisted the other two go back and do the assignment – don't come back to the field until it's complete. Both were back the next day armed with a clearer understanding of their performances and improvement ideas in hand. And more than that, they had the sense of ownership and determination that comes from taking a hard, honest look at oneself.

Rick hadn't known what to expect from his pitchers – his

request was such a radical departure from how he had handled problems in the past. What he got was a new energy and level of engagement from them. They had begun the process of self-actualization – the journey to realize their own potential by discovering what was holding them back.

Rick learned that sharing responsibility with his players resulted in better answers and a higher level of commitment. And it freed him to do other work when they partnered in the creative process with him. Rick and his players shifted from problem solving to talent development.

One important aspect of Rick's story is what it teaches us about creating a framework for players' accountability exercises. First, Rick asked his pitchers to analyze and create accountability from their own experience. He helped them build self-awareness and self-management while still providing clear guidelines and boundaries. He told them, "Watch your films, observe yourself in action and plan for improvement based on what you know. Then let me know your plan and go do it." Rick hadn't given away his power as a coach – he remained the ultimate authority and at the same time, allowed them the opportunity to grow.

Rick knew a lot about pitching. What he didn't know was why each player was getting stuck. He could make assumptions, but as we learned earlier, assumptions are just stories we make up to fill in what we don't know. Out of his frustration of not knowing, Rick asked his players to diagnose their own performance – no assumptions on his part.

In the beginning, the whole approach felt risky. He had never done anything like it before. Initially it had the feeling of giving away his authority as coach. So he was careful to provide structure to what he asked. The players didn't get free rein in their development.

This approach to accountability does not give the foxes free run of the hen house. Rick created boundaries for their accountability and made a clear request to analyze specific behavior. And finally he held them accountable to come back with answers and then execute their plans. Their responsibility was to do the research and then honor their commitments.

This creates opportunities for you to help your athletes help themselves. Historically, coaches have told players what to do then watched to see if assignments were done correctly. In that system, accountability is simply players doing what they are told. When you shift to a conduit approach, you will be asking your players to share in the ownership of what they do. You will partner with your players to help them discover what's working and what's not.

We talked earlier about the work of powerful questions in helping players understand and diagnose what is going on within themselves – this is an ideal place to apply that skill. Once a player realizes ways he or she needs to improve, they will be ready to design their accountability. Conduit accountability is a measurable process to help players mature by asking them to take real responsibility.

A word about players who cannot or will not accept the responsibility offered. It happens. In my world, we teach new coaches that it's not possible to coach someone who doesn't want to be coached. It's true in your world, too. Some players will flourish as you offer them greater degrees of self-actualization. Others will not. They want to be told what to do. Still others will fail – typically through a lack of understanding (they just can't see it) or lack of self-discipline.

Be firm but understanding with the ones who aren't responsive. Make no assumptions but realize that the human brain matures at different rates. It could be that your 19-year-old (or younger) athlete is lacking the brain development required for self-awareness and self-management.

There is one other obstacle for young players. Being responsible may be a foreign idea that needs to be explained. If they've grown up in a world that never allowed them to solve a problem on their own, they may not know how. Be patient and encourage them to learn a step at a time. They will see the success of others and may learn from that. Or not. You job is to remain open, curious and ready.

This approach to accountability and responsibility may well be a recalibration of how you've done things in the past. Accepted practice in sports is that the coach watches athletic performance with an eye for what's going wrong then corrects mistakes so teams win games. If these new ideas feel counterintuitive or too far out to work, remember Rick's experience. The results were profound and set the team on a new trajectory for development. What made it even more profound was how the players' involvement in the process made the changes they practiced stick.

Each athlete owned her own diagnosis and path to corrective action. Rick's job was to add his knowledge of the game to help keep the athletes on track. He offered his expertise as guidance while they owned their results. And they were happy to partner in this new way because of the pride they experienced that comes from achieving success on their own. Change tends to be more permanent when the right person owns the responsibility.

I experienced the delight of discovery and ownership when I sought the help of a golf pro. I couldn't seem to straighten a hook out of my drive. I suspect the pro immediately saw the problem, but she didn't begin by telling me where to move my foot or how to shift my weight. She began by asking me to notice how it felt to swing the club. Then she gave me some clues of what to be aware of in my swing. She helped me sense tension and awkward movement. Then she guided me to self-diagnose my swing while adding her expertise and giving me new things to try. I was delighted to "discover" what I was doing wrong and highly motivated to practice on my own so I could improve my game. The fact that I discovered what needed to be changed fueled my determination. By the way, the only similarity to my golf swing and Jim Furyck's is that we were both allowed to develop one that worked for us!

That's the approach to accountability we are talking about. You aren't leaving your expertise behind – you are just shifting from pure problem solving to sharing responsibility with your player. The more you ask questions to help an athlete understand themselves and solve their own problems, the more they will become involved in the process and can self-diagnose, learn and guide their own development. Great progress can be made to reach an athlete's potential when accountability is self-directed.

Even with the evidence of Rick's experience, you may be full of questions. Why risk trying this approach? Why not just stick with telling people what to do and when to deliver their results? It's OK to ask the questions, but realize the habit of telling people what to do is a telltale sign of only having one tool in your coaching toolkit – one that is not always the best choice.

When *telling* is your primary tool for getting results, you can expect three things -

- First, the other person will do exactly what they're told and then stop and wait for the next instruction.

- Next, they won't tap into their own creativity because you are training them to follow your instructions...and no more.

- Finally, if an idea doesn't work, it's not their fault – it's yours. After all it was *your* idea.

There may be a feeling of control when you tell people what to do, but it's important to also recognize there's a cost. Letting go of control can be challenging –especially in the beginning. But the payoff is self-awareness, creativity and initiative in the people you coach – a true competitive edge.

Rick would tell you that he was amazed and delighted with his results. He would go on to say this approach to accountability and responsibility has become a regular part of his players' development.

His gift to us provides a great example of how to expand range and choices as a coach. You now have an alternative to command and control. The other valuable lesson comes from the players themselves. Most welcomed the opportunity to identify and remove their own barriers and their development happened more quickly.

We've been exploring how accountability looks different in the conduit environment – now let's see how it shifts how we look at responsibility. Imagine a team with a culture of self-discovery and self-improvement. Players come to you with, "Coach, I was noticing I was having a problem with *(fill in the blank for your sport).* Could you take a look and tell me what you think?" As new habits form, players will become responsible for more of their development and production. They will look to you for help in solving performance issues because you've made it safe for them to ask for help. Let's have more of that!

These changes to accountability and responsibility can be culture changing in ways you might not expect. For example, most young athletes are really good at correcting their teammates. Conduit accountability and responsibility has players focus on themselves. If you are committed to including a conduit approach, it becomes a new *way of being* for the individuals and the team. The new default behavior will be for each player to carry their own weight first. It's also a subtle, positive way to deal with dissension in the team because you are replacing blame and accusations with curiosity and a standard of taking responsibility while becoming self-sufficient.

Bringing your team to this place may take time because it's a new, learned skill for coaches and athletes. As their conduit coach, you will hold accountability and responsibility differently. The athlete's job is to create accountability – what work they will do. Your job is to hold them responsible for completing their commitments.

Here's the difference. In command and control, you are looking for tasks to be accomplished. As a conduit, you'll look for results – the culmination of tasks. Accountability in the land of "telling people what to do" is a matter of finding problems and keeping score. There may even be a tendency to assign blame if something isn't completed. Blaming is the next logical step after finding a problem. It's all about scarcity and what's missing or done wrong.

Conduit development, on the other hand, is positive. If things go wrong (or not as planned) in a conduit environment, it is seen as a place for learning, not shaming. The conduit coach offers positive, developmental options rather than blame with questions like, "what did you learn?" or "what has changed?" As a conduit, you and your player work as a team: you are responsible for game smarts, they are responsible for their actions, attitude and work.

A heads up – the relationships you create with this conduit approach will be deeper than might occur otherwise. When you partner in another's development, you get to see the depth of who they are. You'll find that you ask about who they want to become as much as you ask about the mechanics of their play. You'll experience a different tone and energy to your coaching and teaching. And their responses will be different, too. You'll find a lot more excitement and engagement in this approach because self-discovery is an emotionally powerful experience!

When we rolled this kind of self-determination out in business settings, we learned most people thrive in an environment of personal accountability. And if they don't, it provides valuable insight to be able to determine if individuals are a good fit for the culture we want to create.

As a conduit, you offer players the opportunity to own their success. Conduit coach accountability is designed to keep people focused on the goal they envision for themselves and invites creativity into the process. It asks the athlete to be invested in their development – much more than giving them an instruction sheet ever could.

Accountability can be distilled to three questions -

- What are you going to do?
- When will you have it done?
- How will you let me know?

Notice there's a natural order to the questions. The first creates a vision for the future and points to action. The second makes sure something is done - it's measurable. And "how will I know?" closes the loop. Accountability isn't complete without reporting results – good or bad.

Conduit coaching accountability creates a new role for you as the coach. We call it "holding" the accountability. You will ask more questions about what they've learned and less on if they did the task correctly. Notice the diagram below. The relationship of conduit accountability looks like this.

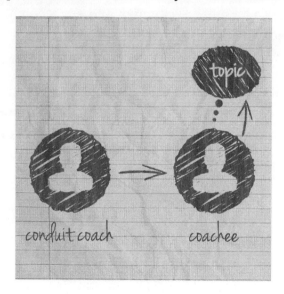

The conduit coach's arrow points toward the coachee, not the topic. It's a visual reminder for us to ask about the player about what they are learning rather than telling them what to do. Questions can sound like, "What did you experience?" "What do you notice?" and "What will you do next?" Your intention is to help the athletes find their own answers. Once an answer becomes clear, you ask, "What will you do? How will you let me know?"

Remember, if the approach isn't working or the player is resistant, you can always shift to giving advice or providing instructions. That's when your arrow will move to point toward the topic.

Consider Rick's story. He didn't know what the players would do when he shifted his approach and asked them to create their own accountability. One player had the courage to try the new approach; the other two thought it might be a trick. They had never been asked to step up and be in charge of their practice before. They were afraid and so they didn't do anything. Thank goodness for the first pitcher who jumped in – even in the face of the unknown! She set the stage for an important change in the team.

Like Rick, the first requirement may be for you to loosen your grip and view accountability as something that can be shared. The second requirement will be to view the results with curiosity rather than judgment. Remember when two pitchers came back empty-handed; Rick's first reaction was to jump down their throats. Instead, he slowed down enough to realize he had thrown them a curve with the assignment. Rather than punishing them for not doing what he asked, he explained the boundaries and the consequences and gave them another chance. He modeled a world of self-determination and responsibility. By the way, he never had to explain it to them again.

Conduit coaching skills may seem counterintuitive in a competitive sporting environment. After all, the coach is the one paid to have the knowledge. Shouldn't you always be the expert? The answer is expert in your *sport,* yes. But your players are the ones who know themselves. And when your goal is to help a player become their best, you want to begin with what is true, not what is assumed. And the only way to learn what's going on in someone's head is to ask. Apply your knowledge, but don't make assumptions – that's the essence of the conduit way.

When you have your conduit coach hat on, there is one more requirement. That is to let go of judgment and blame. On the surface, this may feel counterintuitive, as well, but remember what we said about leaving assumptions behind in an earlier chapter. When someone comes back with incomplete accountability or an unexpected answer, don't assume they screwed up or made a mistake. Instead, be curious. Ask why they made the decisions they did or ask what was missing. In the case of Rick's assignment, what was missing for the students was a bridge. They needed an explanation to help them move from how problems had always been handled to what the coach was asking now. Frankly they didn't trust him, and thought it might be a trick. Once he assured them there was no trick, they left to tackle their assignments.

Have you noticed how self-awareness and self-management are critically important skills for a conduit coach? The better you are with those behaviors, the more you will model them to your organization. Since assumptions, judgment and blame are emotional triggers, emotional intelligence is essential to be able to avoid a rush to judgment. When you are a conduit coach, you have the option to rush to curiosity instead.

Accountability is now more than just a checklist. It is defining and committing to action. Without the step of accountability, conduit coaching is not complete, even if great emotional intelligence, questioning and listening skills have been used. As you begin to practice being a conduit, you'll find that most of the work occurs outside the coaching sessions. That's the importance of accountability. Think of it as an experiential learning tool. It's important to have your athlete articulate what they will do so you can help hold them accountable and stay in touch with their progress.

That leads us to the final element of accountability. It's your responsibility to ask a player what they've done. I was always surprised when my corporate clients told me that it was hard to remember to hold accountability. Follow-up was a challenging leadership skill for some managers! And I've heard all of the excuses – from "I don't have time" to "they should be responsible without my asking," to "once we've moved on, I have a hard time remembering to ask!"

Here's what I learned in business - the coach needs to provide the *discipline* of follow up. It's too easy to assume an assignment was completed and rush off to the next thing. It sounds silly that reminders are even required. After all, if a person makes a commitment, they should remember and execute. And in a perfect world, that's the way it should work. But we are human and change like this can be a real shift! So I recommend a gentle but firm "holding" as they discover their new skills. The discipline will teach them self-awareness and self-management and help reinforce it in you.

It may feel hard to slow down to be a conduit coach. With the sense urgency in your world of wins and losses, it's understandable. But if you take the time to ask, "tell me what you've learned since our last practice," it will tell your athlete that their in-between work matters and that you are aware of their efforts. They will also learn they are ultimately responsible for their actions. They will mature.

You are not only giving your players the opportunity to grow, mature and become more responsible, you give yourself the opportunity to begin to step out of a parental role. Remember, these kids have grown up having to listen to adults and doing what they were told. You are teaching them to think for themselves and become self-sufficient. These skills will serve them well as they play for you and in their lives beyond school and college.

The value around accountability is amazing. Give it a try and it and see what happens. When your players – and any other member of your organization – begin to be personally accountable, you will be freed up to do the things you love the most – coaching your sport. In fact, as accountability becomes an integral part of your organization, you'll find that it is self-perpetuating. The more you encourage others to be accountable, the more accountable they will want to become!

Practice Drills

Creating Accountability

This practice is designed to help you let others create their own accountability. Find a time when you are working one-on-one with an athlete -

- Ask them what they will do to solve their problem, improve the situation or improve their skills.

- Then ask them what support they need.

- Finally ask how and when they will let you know how it worked.

Sharing Responsibility

There are four parts to the practice of sharing responsibility – the first three are ones you've already worked on. Practice these four in order.

1. Be aware of how quickly you want to jump in to tell someone what to do.

2. Don't jump to assumptions.

3. Instead, ask a question of the other person. [Such as, "What do you want for an outcome?" "What's not working?" "What's happening?"]

4. Ask what they would do to change.

Practice these for a week and notice the impact in your organization.

journal page

8

LANGUAGE COUNTS

"What's wrong with you?"
"Don't you get it?"
"You'll never learn!"
"I'm sick and tired of your excuses."

Our language defines our thoughts.
Our thoughts design our behaviors.
Our behaviors create our results.

Sara Smith

Let's take a look at the importance of the words around us.

Think of someone in your life you love to be around. What are the words that come to mind when you think of them - *fun, energetic, loving, trustworthy*? What do those words invite in you?

Now think of someone in your life who is a challenge. As you think of them, what language comes to mind? Is it something like *problem, nosy, know-it-all* or *OMG*? What is your response if I said you will be with them tomorrow?

Notice the words that showed up for you in those two examples. You see how the language we use, even in our thoughts, defines our response to others.

If you are tracking with me in this little exercise, you now have one person in mind you want to have lunch with and one you hope you can avoid. That's what happens when our thoughts design our behaviors. With that as background we're set. Let's take on, *'our behaviors create our results.'*

You may be familiar with the term *naysayer*. They are the people who are ready to offer criticism or tell you what won't work at the drop of a hat. They are chronic critics. A naysayer will rarely offer suggestions or alternatives but is willing to point out the weakness in someone else's idea. If you've ever spent time around this type of energy, you'll agree that the negative attitude and faultfinding can be de-energizing.

The habit of looking for what's wrong or what won't work may stimulate discussion but it also creates a negative environment. For whatever good it brings, it also invites confrontation or retreat in other people.

When a naysayer is present there is often a pattern of shooting down what's being said. When I'm subjected to that, I'll defend new ideas a time or two but then I'll decide it's easier (and safer) to be quiet and keep my ideas to myself. Or if I feel like a target whenever I bring something new or different, I'll quit trying. Notice what happens to creative thinking?

What's interesting is that often "naysaying" is no more than a habit. The naysayer doesn't feel particularly negative. It's just a trap – a habit of looking for problems instead of possibilities. It's an easy pattern to fall into. And the result is an energy that kills creativity and trust.

Sadly, it happens because we humans are hardwired to look for the negative – perhaps it's a tendency is left over from those pre-historic times when there were so many threats to our survival. You'll remember we talked earlier about amygdala hijacks and the importance of knowing our triggers. The impact of the hijack applies here, too. When we habitually use negative language we can unconsciously fire off our own triggers and activate others' just by default word choices and old habits.

Researchers for *Psychology Today* warn us that something as simple as using the word "no" can trigger the neural activity in the brain that releases stress-producing hormones. It's the amygdala hijack we've talked about. They describe it as an interruption of the normal processing of the brain. The interruption impairs logic, reason, language processing and communications. Every time we resort to negativity, we limit ourselves and those around us. Think about it. If you work in a "no" environment, how conducive is it to generating new ideas?

The words we choose offer their own impact. For example, let's take two words often used in sports: tough and mean. We might assume they invoke similar results. In fact, I've heard them used interchangeably. *Tough* and *mean* provide a great point of comparison for us to examine how the words we chose design our behaviors.

Let's start with the differences. *Mean* in this context is about causing trouble or malice for others. When we think of being *mean*, we invite negative responses. Meanness is cruel and threatening and triggers a defensive response. Remember all that's been said about human response to stress? If *mean* shows up, from a coach or other players, it will not inspire people to try to improve. Rather, they will literally or metaphorically run for cover. *Mean* is an energy you want to avoid because when your team is struggling, you want them calm, controlled and able to think – not reeling into an emotional tailspin. The last thing a team needs is for their coach or teammates to send them into a fight, flight or freeze response. Yes, you may want the team to fight their way to victory in the context of a game, but they won't get there with the mind-numbing, shortsighted stress of an amygdala hijack. *Mean* is not a winning strategy.

On the other hand, let's look at *tough*. Tough is being physically and emotionally strong and able to deal with harsh conditions. Let's go a step further to distinguish between the two by seeing how to be tough without being mean. Have you ever raised your voice to warn a child to not touch a hot stove? If so, you've experienced the difference. In that situation, you yell because your intentions are to save another person from harm. That's tough, not mean.

In coaching, *tough* is what happens when you care deeply, want to create lessons and teach responsibility. *Mean* is what comes out when you are angry and want to punish or hurt.

Listen to your language to know the difference. Here is what *mean* sounds like -

- "That was the dumbest thing I've ever seen!" or "What kind of lame choice was that??" *Questioning intelligence*

- "You're killing us!" "Are you playing this way on purpose?" "You're worthless." *Questioning character or intention*

- "Get your head out of your ass!" This one is simply an insult – a cheap shot for a coach to take

The language of anger and punishment can never masquerade as caring or teaching. It may make the one who utters it feel better, but it damages the recipient. Word choice has the power to define and design the speaker. You can choose the demeaning language of a bully or the supportive, disciplined words of a coach.

When you combine EI with what you're learning about language, you will be able to bring a balance of toughness and compassion. The end result will be an organization that is resilient. Your athletes will be challenged in ways that feel safe. They'll know they can try new ideas and make mistakes without being insulted or belittled. And you'll discover another competitive advantage as they become resilient.

Consider what that might mean for your team. By managing the use of negative language to the times when it's really needed, you can actually increase the abilities of your athletes. Sound far-fetched? Here is an example where it did just that.

> *It had been called Hell Week for as long as anyone could remember. It was the week before the beginning of the semester. The coaches loved the time because it provided practice when classes didn't distract the athletes. It was a physical jumpstart to the season.*
>
> *The athletes hated it – after all it was Hell Week. They talked about how hard it was, the long days, the coaches'*

demands. Historically, it was a tense time when patience ran short and tempers were hair-triggered. And as much as the coaching staff loved the opportunity, they realized the cost - everything that went along with the Hell Week theme seemed to carry a price in injuries and bad feelings.

The coaching staff had begun to embrace conduit coaching and wondered if Hell Week could be reframed. So the day the team arrived back on campus, everyone was called into the locker room. The head coach began with, "Let's talk about Hell Week."

The coaches offered athletes some questions to start the discussion. "As you look at Hell Week, what does it make you think of? How does it make you feel?" The team talked about how difficult the week would be. New players voiced caution – maybe even a little more than fear about Hell Week. The coaches talked about their concerns about injuries. They were all hopeful they could use the time effectively, but clearly the players weren't looking forward to an entire week of being driven to the edge of their abilities. Then the coach suggested they rename their week.

Earlier in the year, the team had chosen a theme to guide and motivate them. Their theme was **Bound.** The word reminded them they were bound for a championship year, bound to be accountable to one another and bound to be responsible for their own work and improvement. So when the coaches told them they could make this week whatever they wanted it to be, the team was unanimous – they wanted it to be fun, engaging and they wanted to play. They renamed their time together Bound Week.

When the staff met at the end of Bound Week, they

measured the effectiveness of their new theme. They were amazed. Injuries were down and productivity was up. They had never had a team work harder or be more focused. At the same time, the team met to evaluate their experiences. They were excited with their accomplishments and delighted to be together as a team. They had worked harder, laughed more and made more progress than they ever had during Hell Week.

The only difference between Hell Week and Bound Week was one word. And it was powerful enough to change the tone and outcomes. Their shift in energy and results occurred because everyone was committed to moving from hell to bound. The results were remarkable.

It can really be that simple and that profound.

I do not underestimate how difficult it can be to change habitual language. The words we use can be like old patterns – hard to recognize, harder to break. We know from brain research that it's easier to replace an old neural pathway with a new one than it is to change the old pathway. Since it's easier to create a new habit than to break an old one, let's apply that to language. Our intent is to replace abrasive, confrontational language with words that are positive and constructive. The results will reduce conflict and defensiveness and encourage respect in your organization – like Bound Week.

Let's look around and see where language shows up. Think about your locker room. What are the posted "rules for behavior?" What tone do they set? (And if you don't have a locker room, consider the rules your organization has for the care of uniforms.)

Here is a sign I found online –

LOCKER ROOM SAFETY RULES

- Food, gum, beverages and glass items are prohibited in the locker room

- DO NOT stand on benches

- Running or chasing in the locker room is prohibited

- Snapping of towels at other students is prohibited

- Throwing shoes, books or other objects in the locker room is prohibited

- To prevent loss, damage or personal injury, students should not wear jewelry during physical education

- This school district is NOT responsible for lost or stolen articles

- Lock all valuables in locker and check lock before leaving locker room

- Report all losses and injuries to your teacher or coach

- Please pick up any trash or litter

- Clothing and equipment must be removed from locker on the last day of class

- Anyone found defacing or damaging this locker room will be subject to disciplinary action

This may not be exactly what a sign in your facility might say, but I was just wondering if any of it sounds familiar. What is striking about this list is how it focuses on telling the athletes what can't be done – delivered with a less-than-subtle tone of blame and superiority. You have to get down to the tenth item on the list before anyone thought to say PLEASE. What message does this send? What tone does it set?

Now, imagine a sign in your locker room that emphasizes what can be done in the facility and what championship behavior looks like – signs that sounds helpful and encouraging rather than dogmatic, bureaucratic and rule bound. Remember, whatever message you hang on the wall will greet your athletes every time they walk in. It communicates much more than just rules.

Word choice is critical. When you talk to athletes - or about them – what are you conveying? Does your language suggest that some may not be too bright ("They just don't understand.")? Or perhaps someone is lying ("Really... I thought you said something else"). Have you ever used language that is sarcastic or patronizing? ("You understand, of course, if you don't do the work, you won't make the team.") Even if that last statement *is* true, is it said in a way that gives a player choices or is the tone demeaning?

When we talk about the need for leaders' behavior to be congruent with their messages, it's called *walking your talk*. Look around your facilities, read the memos that go out, listen to what you say to your team. What's your talk? If you are always looking for problems, your words will convey it. It won't be hard to tell if you are focused on what's incorrect or aspiring to what's possible.

Language choice is critical for two reasons. First is that the *command and control* mentality and its associated judgment and blame is deeply imbedded in the culture of sports. Being keenly aware of the language surrounding your organization is vital because negativity can easily become the default.

What's the cost to the organization? Negative thoughts transmitted through negative words have negative consequences. Each time we resort to negativism, we invite the fight, flight or freeze response in others. And studies of human behavior teach us that negative thinking is self-perpetuating – creating powerful neural pathways – and not the ones you want.

The second reason the topic of language is critical is because you have a choice. Your choice and ability to create positive impressions in those you coach is deeply rooted in what we've learned in emotional intelligence.

Let's shift the conversation to look at the impact of positive language. Positive words and thoughts ignite motivational centers of the brain that help build resilience for times we face problems. When you rely on your new skills of self-awareness and self-management to increase your mindfulness, you give yourself the opportunity to choose rather than use default words. Here is a tip - choose your words and then speak them slowly. The pace of your speech will allow you to interrupt the brain's propensity to be negative. And breathe. If the pressure is on or if there is tension in the air, re-oxygenate your brain as your first defense against negativism.

There is power in positive language. Recent research has shown the mere repetition of positive words will turn on specific genes that lower physical and emotional stress. As positive language becomes the organizational norm, your team will benefit physically as well as emotionally. You will invite deeper and more trusting relationships with others.

So where do we go from here? If the impact of words is that profound, let's begin taking advantage of the benefits. Here is a list of negative words and their positive counterparts. You can practice replacing the ones on the left with the words on the right.

Negative Words	Positive Words
No, can't, won't	Yes, can, will
Unacceptable	Acceptable
Hate	Love, Like
Wrong	Right
Hard	Challenging
Should have	Could have
Unfortunately	Fortunately
Always/Never	Often/Seldom
Bad	Unwise
Mistakes	Lessons
Must	Prefer
Faults	Differences
Screw up	Poor choice
	Good, Well done
	Thank you

This list isn't meant to be all-inclusive, just a start to help heighten your awareness of the words that support a positive climate. This will give you the opportunity to recognize and stop habitual negative words before they have a chance to come tumbling out of your mouth, unedited.

In the same way, let's look at some phrases. Again, the intent is to provide options to replace some common, over-used negative phrases with ones that will deliver the message in a positive way.

Replace negative language	With positive language
Yes, but	Yes, and
I'm disappointed	That's disappointing
What were you thinking?	Tell me what happened
This is going to be hard	This could be challenging
You've never gotten it right	Up until now
Let's begin with what didn't work	Let's begin with what worked well

While we are contrasting word choices, let's connect what we are learning about language to the science of emotions. Negative emotions are more contagious than positive ones – it's human nature. We are wired for survival and our default is to be defensive. Because of that, you can count on negative language also being more contagious. The words we choose set the tone for the team.

Dr. John Gottman, relationship expert and author takes the power of language another step for us. He examined negative language and associated the types of behaviors that negativity invites. He refers to the most toxic of those behaviors as the Four Horseman of the Apocalypse. The four are *criticism, defensiveness, contempt* and *stonewalling.* As you grow more aware of the impact of negative language, you'll want to watch for these.

- **Criticism** - blaming or attacking. The language of criticism is full of complaints – and sometimes character assassination. "We have to run extra laps because Jake wasn't running the full length of the field. You can count on him to try to get away with something."

- **Defensiveness** - responding to criticism in a like (defense) manner. Defensiveness is negative and almost always has an element of blame. "It's not my fault, I didn't do anything."

- **Contempt** - belittling others. It is a sign of out of control competitiveness when winning requires subjugating others. The language of contempt includes sarcasm, cynicism, name-calling, hostile humor and belligerence. This is the most poisonous of these four because is conveys superiority and condescension. Contempt is often the birthplace of bullying.

- **Stonewalling** - not actually language, but the fourth toxin is appropriate to the list because it is often the result of negative language. In its mildest form, stonewalling is being reluctant to express opinions directly. Full blown stonewalling can include silent treatments, refusals to engage or withdrawal. This is the same response we described when we talked about the impact of the naysayer.

Why is this list important? I want you to be able to recognize toxic behaviors associated with negative language.

Dr. Gottman's research went on to prove that to create a well performing organization, you need a ratio of 3 positive interactions for every negative interaction. That's for a *good* organization. The ratio for a *great* organization is 5 to 1 – positive to negative. If you want to create a positive culture in your organization the 5 to 1 ratio provides a measurable target for language and behavior.

We began our journey together with *It All Begins with You* and we are coming full circle. Language is a driving force for positive or negative energy in your organization and you'll discover the words you choose are based on where *you* are, Coach. That includes your mood, emotional state and ability to manage your triggers. Understanding yourself is the first hurdle. The next step is to challenge longstanding language and ways of doing things in athletics.

We've talked about the historical approach of correcting mistakes in sports coaching. But if an important key to high performance organizations is a 5 to 1 ratio of positive to negative comments, we need to focus on how to address "mistakes" differently and language is the logical place to begin. We've created the foundation with conduit coaching skills and curiosity. Now let's add a way for you to reframe conversations.

The purpose of the tool I'm about to share is to help you diffuse emotions and conduct developmental conversations in a positive way. It's a way to deal with problems and be intentional about delivering more positive than negative comments.

Let's look at how a conversation between a coach and an athlete often occurs. The coach approaches an athlete to work on a problem and the view of the conversation often looks like this.

Notice the relationship. It's just you and the athlete – mano a mano (that's Spanish for "hand to hand" - as in unarmed combat.) It's a perspective that invites judgment, "Here's what I see you doing wrong." Or from the player's perspective, "the Coach never asks – (s)he always tells me what to do."

Let's play with another approach. Rather than having only *YOU* and the *Athlete* in the picture, we will add a third entity, the *Topic*. The *Topic* is whatever you are working on - a challenge, a new skill or a practice, etc. It's the topic you and your athlete are working on. By adding it to the diagram, we've created a communications triangle. Think of this as the *Conduit Coaching Communications Triangle*.

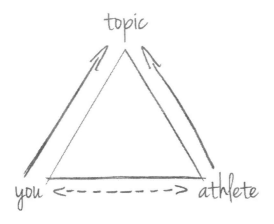

We add the arrows that point from YOU and Athlete up to the Topic. Those arrows suggest a new way to have a conversation. Instead of pointing a comment toward the Athlete, "Here's what I see you doing wrong" which is following the dotted arrow, follow the solid arrow and speak to the topic instead. Here is how the question sounds different –

"You and I are working on securing the ball after it's caught. Tell me how you would evaluate your performance."

Instead of pointing your comment at the player, you point toward the mutual topic – in this case, securing the ball. This conversational technique offers emotional separation between YOU and Athlete without compromising the question at hand. It's an approach that shifts the conversation from *blame and telling* to *collaboration and self-analysis*.

A key difference between the first diagram and the triangle is that the straight-line option defaults to the language of criticism. "Here's what I see you doing wrong…"

While that may be true – the athlete is making a mistake - if the comment triggers a defensive reaction (amygdala hijack), you've already lost your opportunity to help your student self-correct. And that response is likely because defending ourselves when we feel threatened is one of our strongest instincts.

Let's take a look at what happens to your player's ability to accept criticism when you tell them what they are doing wrong. They sense they are being attacked and as you've learned that triggers a neurological response. The amygdala takes over and effectively shuts down the frontal cortex of the brain. When the frontal cortex is deactivated to provide more energy for battle, they are no longer able to effectively take in information. Their vision and attention become narrower as they mentally and physically prepare for attack.

It's not that they intend to shut down – it simply a natural response to stress. At the very time you want your athlete to be open and receptive to information, they are the least prepared because of the effects of an emotional hijack. To say they are no longer open to feedback is an understatement. It's worth repeating that we humans are designed to always be on alert to threats and danger. It is our survival instinct.

So one of the greatest challenges athletic coaches face when offering feedback is when the act of delivering it is perceived as a threat. The fact is – our athletes are human. There is always a risk that feedback might create defensiveness. So what can a coach do? That's why I shared the *Conduit Coach Communications Triangle*. It is a simple approach that diffuses emotions by separating the feedback and the person through the words you use. It allows you to evaluate what you've seen in their performance and report the results. You'll remove (or at least minimize) personal threat and open the door for self-examination and understanding.

With that in mind, let's follow the triangle diagram one more time. I want you to be comfortable separating the topic from your player. When you mentally separate the two you can talk about the situation without the student feeling attacked. By the way, the separation also helps keep you from being triggered if this isn't the first time they've made the same mistake. The person and the topic are treated as different entities through your language.

A statement that separates performance from the athlete might sound like "The serves are well executed in practice but not during the match. What do you think changes?" Rather than, "how come you can nail your serves in practice, but not during a match?" The topic is *serving a tennis ball* – separate and distinct from the player. The first example evaluates results and diffuses emotion then steps into conduit coaching to allow you and your athlete to examine the circumstances with curiosity rather than judgment.

By separating the topic from the person, statements can be definitive about what occurred and you can ask for details without assessing blame. Imagine how different the relationship between coach and player will be when mistakes are met with curiosity rather than judgment and blame.

The triangle diagram demonstrates an approach to tough conversations that maintains respect and civility. If you model following the solid arrows on the triangle, you'll have another tool to train your athletes to be honest and self-aware without fear of automatic criticism. Stay with the solid arrows and know that when situations become tense, avoiding the dotted arrow, (comments like, "What were you thinking?!?") will help discover what actually occurred and how to resolve problems by inviting the player to take responsibility.

Whether it's the language you or your coaching staff use, memos, signs or the chatter allowed in the locker room, the words heard in your organization set the tone for possibilities versus scarcity and respect versus bullying. And you get to choose.

Practice Drills

Go around your facility and read all the signs – also check any manuals and memos or letters that go out from your organization. What is the tone of the communications? Do they sound like guidelines for being part of a high performance organization or rules so people don't get into/cause trouble? Practice re-writing the offensive ones.

One quick language change that helps build self-awareness and self-management is for you to replace "Yes, but" with "Yes and" in your speech.

Here's a quick look at what changes

- *Yes, but* means, "I heard what you said and now I'm going to correct you."

- *Yes, and* says, "I am going to build on what you said."

The use of "yes, but" is common and often unconscious. This simple word swap has the potential to bring profound change to your organization.

The next time you work with a player, practice using the Conduit Coaching Communications Triangle to talk about the topic in a way that is healthy and collaborative.

journal page

9

CELEBRATION!

"The more you praise and celebrate in your life, the more there is to celebrate."

Oprah Winfrey

Celebration is more than just a banquet at the end of season. When you are a conduit for success, celebration is also the atmosphere you create. Benjamin Zander, in his book, *The Art of Possibilities* teaches us, "Draw a different frame around the same set of circumstances and new pathways come into view. Find the right framework and extraordinary accomplishment becomes an everyday experience." You want great success, so let's practice *drawing a different frame.* You can create an environment where success is anticipated, looked for and celebrated.

In fact, I invite you to see your purpose as a coach and conduit to create an organization that is resilient and thrives on possibilities and progress. That's a winning culture. To make resilience stick takes reinforcement. It requires you to draw a different frame – one that is intentional, positive and celebratory.

We often consider celebrations to be big events with invitation lists and refreshments. Let's reframe celebrations – the art of celebrating in a more holistic way. Think of celebration as a positive *way of being* that actively recognizes and celebrates progress as well as major accomplishments. If the thought of non-stop celebration feels unnatural, perhaps naïve, I get it. It may feel like a dramatic change, but it's a natural step to the EI work you've been doing.

Let's go back to the tradition of the coach's job being to fix problems and correct mistakes. That is a model of scarcity and teaches the organization that the world is a place of want where there is never enough. Yes, there are problems that need correcting, but as you build an emotionally intelligent organization, fixing problems is only one area of focus. You work equally hard (or harder) on development and creating possibilities.

Imagine your organization majoring in possibilities and development and minoring on what's broken. Celebration will help. It is a skill that builds an organization that's hungry to learn and improve, always looking for what's possible.

The first step toward creating a culture of celebration is to systematically take time to look at progress from a strategic perspective. That means you need to get out of the trenches. It's hard to see much more than the side of the trench from down there.

Let's borrow a page from football's playbook. During a game, the staff on the field relies on the perspective of the coach in the press box. He's the one with the best view of what's going on – good and bad. So let's go up into your press box and see what a new, broader perspective offers. This is the initial step to shift from 'looking for problems' mode and into celebration mode.

When you are up in your press box, begin by asking the question, "What do I want for my organization?" Don't settle for just wanting a championship season. That's a given. Let that *want* just be the beginning. I invite you to allow the question 'what do I want?' point beyond X's and O's. What do you want for your athletes – for their lives? What do you want your legacy to be? The view can be expansive up here in the press box.

So the first skill of celebration is to get off the practice field and up into the press box. It's a simple matter of remembering to get out of the rut of details on a regular basis. If you only inhabit the valley of running plays you risk getting stuck in a tactical perspective. In the same way, if team development is only measured from the "field" point of view, performance is never good enough. From down there, all we can see is what's in front of us. We see pitchers letting go with wild pitches, an offensive line collapsing or a defense that doesn't have enough left in the tank by the end of the game. From the field perspective, people always need more development and the work is never done. True as that is, stop for a minute and check out how heavy and negative it feels to dwell on those thoughts.

Now let's go back up to the press box. From here you can see where the team began and how far they've come. You can see how hard individuals work. You'll see the added effort some athletes always seem to put in to reach their best. From this altitude, you can look toward the horizon and see what's possible for your group of talented players. From here, the pitcher had one wild pitch out of 30, the offensive line missed one assignment and the defense needs to understand how to manage energy along with their emotions. Pause for just a minute and notice what happens when you change perspectives. By the way, if you hear a little voice whispering "yes, but there is still a lot of work to do," in this is a perfect time to try, "yes AND there is still a lot of work to do." Notice the energy shift. You are in the neighborhood of celebration.

We are moving away from the energy of work being hard and uphill – that tactical view where you can only see what's not complete and what's missing. A shift up to the press box offers a more expansive view that includes bigger space, more time and hope. Both views of the field contain the same athletes in the same circumstances. What changes is framework and that can change how we choose to see them.

So celebration begins with the ability to get off the practice field and up to the press box. The second step is to share what you see from up there with others. When you celebrate, you invite your organization to join you in a positive place. To keep a team positive and energized, they need to be regularly reminded of where they've been, how far they have come and the progress they are making.

Celebration is an energy that you and your staff can bring to the organization. It is the skill of looking for what's going right rather than focusing on what is wrong. When we started talking about celebration, I described it as a "way of being." Creating a positive way to be in the world is a powerful concept. You've seen how the energy you bring to the organization sets the tone for others. When you are positive you invite positivity. When you are angry, you invite churn. The more you model celebration, the more the organization will emulate being positive and be able to see a bright future. As you lean toward what's possible rather than what's missing, they will, as well. That's what my friend Max learned.

Max is a head coach who called me in when he realized something had to change. Every time he and his staff debriefed a practice the conversation always seemed to end up a gritch session, (A 'gritch' is the combination of griping and bitching - offering the worst of each).

The target of their comments could be the athletes, trainers or administration – everyone was fair game! They had gotten into a habit of scarcity. No one was ever good enough and life wasn't fair. The staff meetings had become a gathering of victims. One of the biggest problems with their gritching was it set the tone for entire the program. As you've learned, when leaders feel like victims, those feelings will telegraph throughout the organization. And before you know it, mediocrity and lack of responsibility become the norm. Why 'lack of responsibility?' Easy. If I'm a victim, whatever is wrong is not my fault – so how can I be responsible?

Let's get back to Max; He knew they needed a change. We began the process of replacing a negative habit with a positive one. Their first step was to understand what was happening – to recognize their default of complaining. The staff agreed to change the tone of their meeting. They replaced looking for problems with looking for things that were going right.

It didn't take long before they began to find more possibilities and hope. They learned the more they looked for what was good, the more they found. The next step was to communicate the hope and possibilities to their team in the form of celebration. The benefits grew exponentially. The more the staff celebrated success, the more successes began to show up in the team.

That's the way it works; the more you look for positives, the more there will be to discover. One obvious reason for that is the team responded to the new energy. They liked how it felt to be recognized and wanted to be the one noticed and praised. Most of the players amped up their work to become the point of celebration. Even the laggards began to follow.

Your next question may be, "What does this celebration stuff look like? I have limited time and budget."

Let's get to the behaviors that create a culture of celebration and positive energy. First, take time to notice and celebrate small victories. Have you asked a pitcher to clean up a slider and they did? Celebrate. Did the offensive unit click today better than usual? Celebrate. Is the team exceeding expectations – ready to start practice on time, taking care of the locker room, genuinely supporting one another? Don't just notice and nod. Smile, thank someone, give a pat on the shoulder. Celebrate.

It's really simple. A spirit of celebration can be shared with a word or a tap on the back. It can be a quick comment in a team meeting, a "thumbs up" or anything that communicates, "I saw what you did and know what you've overcome to get there. Hooray for you!"

When I worked in business, we spent time studying the impact of positive reinforcement. Remember when I said that a great organization provides positive to negative at a ratio of five positive comments for every negative one? We learned that positive responses are easy to create. It just takes awareness and intention. For example, when someone walks into the room and you look up and smile, that's a positive response. If you ignore them, it's a negative response. Smiles, thank you's and calling people by their name are all positive responses. I also like high five's and fist bumps. You can choose whatever is popular this season. The more you invest time and effort in being positive and celebration, the more it becomes your *way of being*. With practice it will be easy to attain the 5 to 1 positive to negative response ratio of a high performance team.

The bottom line is that a staff that holds celebrating success as a value will be on the lookout for what's working and reasons to celebrate. It's another way to model a positive *way of being* for your team. It's all a matter of attitude and attitude is the fuel that makes the unexpected possible and can be the difference between a winning and losing season.

There is one more reason to focus on the positive. This is a story that Dr. Carol Kaufman of the Harvard University School of Medicine told a group of executive coaches. She was teaching us the power of positivity and shared the results of studies that had been conducted on positive reinforcement. As part of the work, researchers began by bringing in two groups of students to take a written test. The same type of students comprised both groups and the tests were identical. What was different was the set up - what they said to each group as they came into the testing center. The first group was thanked and told, based on the type of students they were, the test should be easy – no problem at all. The second group was also thanked. Then they were told this test would likely be a stretch for them but to try and do their best.

When the results were in, the positively reinforced group outperformed their negatively reinforced colleagues – by an average of one letter grade. The researchers tried their experiment again – several times - with a variety of test groups – always equal in capability. It didn't matter what the gender, ethnic or socio-economic level was tested. In equally capable students, the results were always the same. Hope for success always delivered better results.

If you create a culture of celebration, it will bring positive energy with it. To make it happen, start with looking for what's positive and talk about it. The payoff is significant.

Here are some helpful tips for creating that culture -

- Make it a point to metaphorically get off the practice field and up into the press box. Get a strategic perspective on a regular basis. You won't want to stay up there all the time, but that's where you'll get the best the view of success.

- Look for what's going right even as you are looking for what's not working.

- Celebrate what is working – especially if you know someone has focused effort on making it right.

- Remember a celebration can be simple. It can be a pat on the back or an affirmative comment. Make sure you celebrate with individuals as well as with the entire team.

- Begin reviews or debriefs with what went right before jumping into what went wrong.

- Reduce victimhood – in yourself and others. It's a debilitating perspective. Be ready to ask, "What *is* in your control? What can you do about it?" Don't accept 'nothing' or 'I don't know' as an answer. You can always ask, "What *do* you know?"

Be aware that you'll need to personally invest in being positive. This is not a place where you can "fake it till you make it." Your emotions and the energy you feel are transmitted to others. Don't act like you are delighted when you are not – people will sense the duplicity. This is a time to look for what's right and let it delight you. Be honest with yourself so you can be honest with your team. It is the emotionally intelligent way.

Acknowledgement

One last powerful skill of celebration I want to share with you is *acknowledgement.* An acknowledgement is a comment that recognizes the inner person. More than what they did, an acknowledgement highlights who they had to be to accomplish the task – the character they displayed.

Here are some examples

> *When a quarterback stands in the pocket and completes the pass: "Scott, you showed real determination when you didn't let that defensive line shake your confidence. You reached deep!"*

> *When a soccer player challenges the opposition for a pass: "Janise, you were heroic when you stepped in front of the midfielder to intercept their pass. You really showed your commitment to winning."*

> *When an outfielder makes a courageous, athletic catch: "Your fitness is amazing. You've invested a lot of hours the rest of us don't see."*

> *When a second string player works harder than their first string counterparts: "I can see your competitive passion in this."*

Acknowledgement is not a compliment. A compliment highlights what someone did like, "Great job getting past those blockers!"

Acknowledgement is also not praise like "You're doing a better job keeping your body aligned during your serve."

It's not an opinion, "Your leadership on the field is an inspiration to me."

Compliments, praise and high opinions are good, but acknowledgements are even more powerful.

The skill of acknowledgment celebrates internal strengths. When you acknowledge someone's character, you help that person see what they might miss (or dismiss) in themselves. Being able to acknowledge means you have to practice looking deeper than a player's physical effort. You need to see who that other person is being – or becoming - to reach their success.

When you acknowledge someone, you give them permission to tap more fully into the strength you see. When they hear you articulate their strengths out loud, you help them become even stronger. You give them the support to be unexpectedly successful. Here is the impact of acknowledgement on an unlikely candidate for a basketball standout.

> *He was too short to play basketball. Everyone said so. But Bill loved the game and he knew he could shoot. At 5' 7", no high school coach would look at him. But there was a one coach – a volunteer at the Boy's Club. When he looked at Bill, he saw possibilities. So they began to shoot together. This part-time, untrained coach cheered for Bill and reminded him that his "heart and hustle" made him 6' 6." Bill learned he could believe it because his coach said so. It*

gave him the courage to join his high school's basketball program.

Bill didn't get to play until the first string point guard got sick in the middle of the first half of a game. When Bill stepped in, he had the words of his mentor in his head, "heart and hustle." By the end of the game, Bill had scored 20 points. By the end of the season, he was averaging 26 points a game and was named Player of the Year and made the All-State team. In a world of tall players – and bias in favor of being tall – Bill became a 5' 7" star.

Acknowledgment goes straight to the heart. It sees what the other person values, where they are growing and often fills a need for validation. When you acknowledge someone, you partner with him in his success.

To be successful at acknowledging others, there are two parts to practice.

- The first part is delivering the acknowledgement. Take time to deliver it – don't let it be an off-hand comment.

- The second part is noticing the impact on the other person.

This step is important because the other person may shrug it off – don't let that happen. We humans aren't used to being really seen. Part of your job is to train the other person to receive your message. You can do that by helping them stop and just take it in. "I really mean it" can go a long way.

A great acknowledgment will land in a way you can hear, sense and see in the recipient. It is enormously moving for people to be seen and known in this way. And though it may take practice – and a lot of paying attention on your part - it is a valuable tool for a conduit coach.

Here are some ideas for acknowledgements

- You are the heart of this team

- I saw your courage

- You are a hard worker

- You are dedicated

- You are a great teammate

- You are a champion

- I know you dug deep to get that shot

One last word about celebration - remember, creating a positive way of being for your organization begins with you, Coach. The more you offer a positive tone, the more that tone will become part of the fabric of your organization. I tell my leader clients that the ultimate measure of success is when members of your team bring their best game to every aspect of the program – even when no one is watching. That's the ultimate payoff!

Practice Drills

Celebration

Spend a day making notes on what is going right. Look everywhere in your organization from the team manager planning for travel, to an athlete who comes in early to get a little more time in the weight room. And thank them. They will notice that you've noticed. Remember, what is rewarded is repeated.

Begin the practice of mentioning what went well before jumping into what needs to be corrected. It will give you ideas of what to celebrate. Try asking players to share what they saw that worked in a practice or game. It will teach them to celebrate and help them to get up in the press box, too.

Acknowledgement

Find 5 people to acknowledge today. Here are some places to look

- Notice the extra-milers. The ones who never slack – even when no one is looking. They are dedicated.

- Notice the experimenters. The ones who keep trying new ways to get better. They are creative, the innovators.

- Notice the ones who refuse to join in a group running someone down or who will speak up when everyone else hangs their head or avoids eye contact. They are courageous.

journal page

10

BALANCE: THE ROAD TO RESILIENCE

"Balance; that's the secret. Moderate extremism. The best of both worlds"

Edward Abbey

"It is not the strongest of the species that survive, not the most intelligent, but the one most responsive to change."

Charles Darwin

Balance is what is happening when you are triggered and are able to recover. It's also your ability to see more than one option. And it is being able to choose among your options rather than simply reacting to the circumstances around you. Balance is what is happening when you choose among being tough or compassionate, teacher or conduit. When a team experiences balance in their coach, they can be courageous and creative because they aren't afraid of reprisals. They are confident because you believe in them and they know you have their back. They experience balance and are able to be resilient and responsive when faced with the unknowns of competition.

The lessons of emotional intelligence allow you to *be* different as a coach – not just to act differently. The competencies you've learned open the door to balance, resiliency and competitive strength. It is a strength that you'll have at the cellular level as emotional intelligence becomes integral to every fiber of your being.

Balance comes with knowing yourself and understanding how circumstances impact you. It's the ability to be able to see and choose among alternatives. You'll encounter students like Kayla, the player whose mother was ill, or other players or situations that would have pushed your buttons in the past. Balance is realizing you have a choice and can choose between being a hard-nosed coach or a conduit coach.

Let's create a framework for balance. The best example I know is Nik Wallenda, the tight ropewalker who successfully crossed Niagara Falls, the Grand Canyon and downtown Chicago on a cable. As he steps into the slippery unknown without the benefit of a safety tether, he holds a long pole for balance. He relies on his balance pole as it shifts and moves based on the conditions. If you watch Wallenda closely, you see enormous concentration and respect for the elements surrounding him. Like Nik, you are called to be aware, respectful and to find that sweet spot of balance in shifting circumstances.

Let balance serve as a reminder that you have choices. When you exercise your skills of self-awareness and self-management, you are allowing yourself time to operate from a more objective, emotionally intelligent point of view. Your EI skills provide better short-term results as well as improved long-term results for you and your team.

Imagine that you are holding your own long pole for balance.

Command and control is at one end and conduit coaching is at the other. In the middle, you'll find your balance. It's the best place for you to operate. When the environment shifts one way, you chose to ask a question. When it blows from another direction, you can choose to be firm. That's balance.

When we think or the daredevil's pole, balance is the ability to recognize the possibilities that come with a variety of choices. Balance in coaching is more than just being a drill sergeant or relinquishing control. When you are balanced, you can move out of "either/or" to "both and."

When people are used to reacting they often see only two choices – 'either or'. It's like a newspaper story I read. In it, a coach we'll call Joe shared that he had been in a good mood for the last two years. His team had moved into a new and bigger conference, and the school had inaugurated a new stadium. But now, the story went on to report, he didn't want to be in too much of a good mood because the team needed to focus on winning.

Interesting perspective. He believes that a bad mood might be more conducive to winning. I don't know if Coach Joe actually said that and frankly, it doesn't matter. What is important is recognizing that misconceptions can cloud our thinking and lead us to jump from one extreme to another. It's another impact of language. If you aren't thoughtfully engaged, it might be easy to jump to the conclusion that if you are not nice, you must be mean or that a good mood is "soft" and a bad mood is "serious and focused."

Coach Joe isn't the first one to misunderstand those choices. I've worked with executives in IBM and other corporations who believed they could only be kind and hopeful when business was going well. But when the numbers turned down, the leader had to become mean, heartless and inconsiderate – basically transform into a jerk.

Misunderstandings like that lead us astray – like thinking that *mean* is the opposite of *nice* or that being in a bad mood is a prerequisite to getting the best from a team. Since we know emotions are contagious, we know being in a bad mood is likely to create an atmosphere of uncertainty and suspicion. That is not the path to a championship season. In fact we need to discredit the idea that if we are serious about winning, we have to be rough, mean and may have to occasionally resort to bullying; that is simply not true.

Marcus Buckingham, in his book *Go Put Your Strengths to Work*, reminds us to beware of the "opposites trap." For example, he pointed out that the opposite of success is not failure. He implores leaders not to study failures hoping to find the path to success. He warns that if we study failure, we'll end up knowing all the details about how to fail. He goes on to say that if we want to be successful, study success.

You can follow that logic with your team. If you want effective teaming, don't be a bully or you'll develop a team that has no respect. If you want a great team, choose to be clear, firm and consistent. Balance for an emotional intelligent coach is determining how to be firm, tough and curious simultaneously. It's not a choice between nice and mean. Coaches who resort to meanness or bullying are likely in the throes of an amygdala hijack – emotionally out of control and certainly not in balance. When you operate from a place of balance, you don't need to be a bully to get results.

Balance understands there are no short cuts. There can also be misconceptions about how to get a team energetically "up" for a game. I read one story about a college quarterback who didn't get it right. He was just learning to run a hurry-up offense. If you're not familiar with what that, it's an offensive strategy that increases the pace of the game. There is no time for huddles or for the defense to recover and reset between plays.

The young quarterback was being called on to maintain a high level of physical readiness and energy all the time. He was finding the energy, but was beginning to have emotional control problems on the field. The problems were showing up as unsportsmanlike conduct penalties – things like spiking the ball and pushing opponents after the whistle. His coach stated, "As a quarterback, he needs to learn to keep his emotions under control."

Here's where the idea of balance comes in. It's likely that our quarterback was taking the easiest path to being in a sustained, high-energy state. If he worked up to a game-time emotional frenzy, he experienced the stress chemical cocktail that accompanies an amygdala-induced response. That means he relied on cortisol and other stress response chemicals in his system to provide energy to operate at peak levels for long periods of time.

What is sacrificed by that approach is emotional self-control; the ability to think rationally and control behavior in a way that's balanced. He would be producing the levels of energy required but at a significant cost. Even his coach agreed the officials were making the right calls against him. Rather than rely on stress, the young athlete needs to find the balance between high energy and being in control. It's common sense, but the common practice can be challenging especially if our player doesn't know what you now know about the biology of self-control. Since you know the science of emotions you can guide your team to perform with high (but balanced) levels of energy.

Balance is the culmination of all the other lessons we've covered. It's the centerpiece of emotionally intelligent leadership. So here is your roadmap to success:

- The **first** road sign is one emblazoned with the word "choice." When it feels as though you need to react, stop and realize you have a choice. You have learned the skills of self-awareness. Before you react, you can notice your triggers. Breathe and step back to manage them. Remember Rick, the pitching coach - he was stumped when *telling* didn't work until he realized he could ask the players to find their own solutions.

- The **second** mile marker is self-management. This is your ability to see more than one path or behavior. You get to intentionally choose rather than default to old behaviors. If Mike Rice, basketball coach at Rutgers had recognized this signpost, he might have chosen a path different from one of throwing balls and insults.

- The **third** marker is your ability to see others and their situations differently. It's your social intelligence. You are now aware of how assumptions begin to weave their tale of fantasy into your thoughts. You know that assumptions also color your perceptions of reality. Becoming emotionally intelligent transforms how we see the world because we've changed the lens through which we look. Situations we encounter become less emotionally charged, and we can see more possibilities.

Kayla's coach, Jim was ready to read her the riot act about her lousy practice until he paused and realized he was making assumptions. He chose instead to ask a question. And it changed everything.

- The **fourth** and final milestone to keep you on the path to balance is taking time to notice how people respond differently. Conduit coaching invites those around you to be more creative, mature and accountable. One thing to expect as you change your interactions with others is you will change their world. A high performance climate creates stability, clarity and resilience. Your players won't need to invest their energy wondering what will set you off next. They won't feel like they have to watch their backs. When you model emotionally intelligent behavior, they will learn EI, as well. You'll find that your organization will begin to reflect your balance.

As these signposts become more familiar, you'll find yourself discovering more options, responding rather than reacting. You will see situations and people differently. You'll notice that the people around you respond differently, too.

The more you recognize old default reactions, the more you will be able to make different choices - especially when times get tough. If your default has been to yell or tell players to drop and give you 50 when they make mistakes, you now can find other options.

When the game plan isn't working is the very time you want to telegraph calm not frantic emotions to the team. It's important to recognize that times of stress are when negative emotions are the most contagious. You've seen it in the locker room when one belligerent player torpedoes the energy of the entire room. As their leader, your emotional state is vitally important to the "climate" of the team. Your job, when things get tough, is to be the calm in the storm, not the storm. When you keep the team on an even keel, you gain a competitive advantage.

As you contemplate leading from a place of balance consider the possibilities. You will be able to so do much more than just steer clear of blow-ups. When emotional intelligence is your operating norm, you have the tools to find the positive potential in any circumstance. One of the greatest advantages to working in balance is the realization that there are lots of possibilities – even in hard times. The skill is to pause so you can see them.

In my type of coaching, we call that place of possibilities *abundance.* The culture of athletics traditionally sees the world as a place of scarcity – a team that's not practicing hard enough, a player who is not getting out of the block cleanly, a schedule that's unfair. As you notice the impact of negative language, remember the naysayer. Even if all the examples are true, there does not have to be hopelessness.

Looking at life through the lens of what is wrong is the essence of scarcity. One of the risks of relying solely on that viewpoint is that we adopt the mentality of a victim – a victim of the team's laziness, the player's ability or the cruelty of fate. Take a moment to notice the energy. When we are victims, someone else is in charge and we can't control our circumstances. When a coach feels like a victim – intentionally, unintentionally or habitually — the energy of scarcity can ripple through the entire organization. Everyone will feel the emotion that's been triggered in you. You never want your team to get a "hopeless" vibe, especially from you.

When you recognize your emotional triggers, you can manage your emotions and redirect your energy. Rather than getting hooked you now have the tools to diffuse the emotions. Then you can choose to examine the uninspired team or the slow response of the runner or the tough schedule. You can view the circumstances as data and use the data to determine your options. So much more is available when you aren't triggered.

You've set the stage to be open to possibilities. That's where the perspective of abundance comes in. By getting off the playing field, you can see the landscape of possibilities from the strategic perspective of your personal press box. Possibilities become choices and they are the keys to creativity and success. Just believing that there are choices to be found will replace feelings of desperation with hope.

The more you see abundance and potential, the more your team will, as well. Your ability to be positive gives them the gift of possibility and resilience. And you will discover that an emotionally resilient team is one that can recover when they are knocked off their center.

You've seen it before. The difference between winning and losing a game is often the player's/team's ability to keep their heads about them when things go wrong. If you've coached for very long, you've experienced the resilience of a team when a key player provides positive energy to correct the direction of the team when the game goes off course. When you've seen that, you have seen balance in action. As an emotionally intelligent coach, you will be able to offer an anchor to those around you so they can recover when emotions would try to wash them away.

There will be times, at least in the beginning as you practice these new skills, when it may feel like you are stepping into the unknown. You can be confident, the more you practice EI, the more finely attuned you will become to the world around you. You'll find the more you exercise *noticing* – that's a word you've heard a lot in the practice drills – the more you will be able to sense and observe.

The same scientific work that showed us that emotions are contagious teaches us that as we exercise our emotional-attunement, the more we are able to sense in the people around us. It's been called intuition. Brain research shows that our neural wiring is designed to allow us to pick up subtle signals from one another. We have high-speed neuron-based connections of emotions, beliefs and judgments that create our social guidance system. The skills of self-awareness and self-management are the foundation for being able to perceive and connect beyond what is obvious in the world.

It's an ability that's been around for as long as humans have walked the earth. So whether you call it intuition or a gut feeling, it is real and available. You may find your inner sense to be a reliable source of information as you become attuned and emotionally aware.

As an emotionally intelligent conduit coach, you will create a new field of play, one that is balanced, resilient and allows people to recover, even if their emotions sometimes get the best of them. You can confidently let go of the concept that the head coach must be the sole authority in all things, the one who has all the answers and sacrifices everything for the sake of the game. You now have collaboration, shared accountability and responsibility and a new role available called conduit coaching.

One last, gentle warning – there may be those who assume EI

somehow means you've gone soft. On the contrary, I've been a professional coach in major corporations for over a dozen years and I've seen that the strongest leaders are the ones who have the *hard* knowledge of the business and the *soft* skills to get the best from their people.

As we said at the beginning, the truth is, if you are going to be successful, Coach, it will be through the efforts of others. Being emotionally intelligent is a winning strategy because being able to control your emotions, use them effectively and model and teach the skills in your organization is anything but soft. These are complex human relationship skills – not for the wimpy or half hearted!

The bottom line is that you are measured in wins and losses and a lot of your decisions must be made through thorough analysis of the statistics. But the other side of the sports coaching equation is that all of the stats and wins occur through the efforts of others.

Your ability to get the best out of others can make all the difference. It can shift a losing season into a winning one; it can transform the attitude of a single player or the entire web of your organization to see possibilities instead of scarcity. It can provide the resilience to persevere even when it gets hard.

It can change everything.

Practice Drills

Opposites

Take a day and become aware of your use of word opposites. For example – do you think of a player as uncooperative vs. cooperative? What if those aren't really opposites? Be curious because as you know, the words you choose often define your response. (By the way, the opposite of cooperative may be *confused*)

Balance

The practice of balance is the culmination of all you've learned. Breathe deeply and jump into the deep end of the pool – you have what you need to swim confidently.

journal page

Post-Game Analysis

After every game, the team gathers to watch films, review what happened and assess what's been learned. In the spirit of the post-game analysis, I wanted to provide end notes, additional explanations and background. If you like the ideas and want to know more, you'll find references and a *Further Reading* list of the books and articles with ideas that were used in writing *Coach to Coach: Emotional Intelligence and Leadership for Winning Coaches.*

Chapters 3 - Emotional Intelligence – Stats for Success

and

Chapter 4 – Learning Emotional Intelligence

Thanks to Dr. Daniel Goleman and the consultants at the Hay Group of Boston Massachusetts (www.haygroup.com) for concepts included in the Emotional Intelligence models. Goleman is the originator of the EI model in his book *Emotional Intelligence* and collaborated with The Hay Group to create competencies and methods for measuring emotionally intelligent behaviors. I began my learning journey with the Hay Group in their ESCI (Emotional & Social Competencies Inventory) coach training.

If you are interested in measuring your emotional intelligence, you may want to consider investing in an EI survey. These instruments are typically administered by a professional coach or counselor and are often web-based. There are a lot of surveys on the market and I would recommend finding one that is research-based. Here are four that are reputable. They measure and compare your behaviors against a database of others' responses.

1. Emotional and Social Competency Inventory (ESCI), the Hay Group

2. The Social + Emotional Intelligence Profile (SEIP), Laura Belston

3. EQ-I 2, Bar-On;

4. EQ Map, Orioli and Cooper

Chapter 5 – Taking These Skills to Work

I wanted you to think of the skill of listening differently – not as just "on" or "off" - so I began with the construct of Levels of Listening and Levels of Awareness. That idea comes from the core coaching competencies defined by the International Coach Federation (www.coachfederation.org). I also borrowed ideas from *Co-Active Coaching: Changing Business, Transforming Lives*, a coaching manual (for professional and life coaches) written by Henry Kimsey-House, Karen Kimsey-House, Phil Sandahl and Laura Whitworth, 2011. When you approach listening as different levels of awareness, you are able to understand the depth of emotional intelligence. These practices are design for you to into abilities that humans are wired for – which leads me to recommend a short but valuable work on the science of emotional intelligence,

In 2008, Richard Boyatzis and Daniel Goleman, colleagues in the exploration of emotional intelligence in leadership, authored the groundbreaking Harvard Business Review, *Social Intelligence and the Biology of Leadership*, Harvard Business Review by Daniel Goleman and Richard Boyatzis, September 2008, R0809E. In it, Goleman and Boyatzis combine the recent revelations in brain research with leadership theory to provide an easy to understand explanation of the science, married with teaching it's potential for leaders.

Chapter 6 – The Journey to EI

If you are intrigued by how just being curious increases brain activity, positive chemical responses and creativity, read "Energizing Curiosity in Your Innovative Brain", The Innovative Brain newsletter, www.newandimproved.com

Chapter 8 – Language Counts

There is more research being done about the neuropsychological impact of language all the time. You can read more about the science behind positive language and its emotional impact in others in the article, 'Words Can Change Your Brain", Andrew Newberg, M.D. and Mark Robert Waldman. Psychology Today, 2012

If you wonder how to go about seeing others in a generous, positive way, I recommend *The Anatomy of Peace* by The Arbinger Group. It is a learning parable based on the work of Martin Buber. Buber studied the differences between *I/Thou* and *I/It* relationships. The Anatomy of Peace calls the difference - seeing people as *people* versus seeing them as *objects*. The book offers an easy to understand (and relate to) story explaining a complicated concept.

It may seem logical – or maybe not – the ways positive thoughts can make such a difference. According to Sonja Lyubomirsky, one of the world's leading researchers on happiness, if you want to develop lifelong satisfaction, you should regularly engage in positive thinking about yourself, which includes sharing your happiest events with others, and savoring every positive experience in your life. You can read more of her research and conclusions in *The How of Happiness: A Scientific Approach to Getting the Life You Want.* New York, NY; Penguin Press, 2008.

As important as it is to understand the power of positivity, it's equally critical to recognize the power of being negative. That's why I included the work of Dr. John Gottman. He is a recognized expert in the field of relationships and marriage. Gottman developed what he calls his "Four Horsemen of the Apocalypse" for healthy relationships. They are the four categories of bad behavior that can become chronic in dysfunctional teams. I used an interpretation of his work, *The Top 4 Toxic Behaviors in Relationships* developed by Fernando Lopez for the Center for Right Relationships. I like it because it nets out what to watch for so you can nip bad tendencies in the bud!

I wanted to provide a visual aid for you to *see* how to direct a conversation to diffuse emotions in you and the one you are talking with so I created the *Conduit Coaching Communications Triangle*. It is an idea adapted from The

Coaching Triangle taught by The Coaches Training Institute (CTI). The triangle is an easy model that provides a way to envision having tough conversations that deliver a hard message without being unnecessarily hard on the person. In my work we call it delivering a hard message without being harsh.

Chapter 9 – CELEBRATION!

I am indebted to Dr. Carol Kaufman, PhD, PCC and founder of the Harvard Institute of Coaching. She is a world-class scholar on human behavior and became a coach because she was curious about the profession and wondered if it could really produce the results that were being touted. She chose to become a credentialed coach and then begin to study and understand coaching from the inside. She presented to a roomful of coaches at the International Coach Federation International Conference in 2006. She introduced us to research in positivity - the impact of positive languages and affirmations. That was the story about students and their high rates of success in written exams when they received positive affirmation before beginning. Carol told us, "I've learned the power of the work you do by becoming a coach. Now it is my job to prove it through research." What an ally!

Finally, thanks to The Coaches Training Institute (CTI), which named and teaches the coaching skill of *acknowledgment*. Much like breaking listening into 3 unique parts, they have taken the skill of recognizing and articulating someone's character and separated it from giving a compliment or praise. By doing so, they provide us one more valuable skill to motivating others. You can learn more about *acknowledgements* in *Co-Active Coaching: New Skills for Coaching People Toward Success in Work and Life*, Laura Whitworth, Karen Kimsey-House, Henry Kimsey-House and Phillip Sandahl, 2007.

Further Reading

Buckingham, Marcus. *Go Put Your Strengths to Work: 6 Powerful Steps to Achieve Outstanding Performance.* New York, NY: Free Press, 2007.

Goleman, Daniel, *Emotional Intelligence.* New York; Bantam Books, 1995.

Goleman, Daniel, Richard Boyatzis. *Social Intelligence and the Biology of Leadership.* Boston: Harvard Business Review, Harvard Business School Press, 2008.

Goleman, Daniel, Richard Boyatzis and Annie McKee. *Primal Leadership: Realizing the Power of Emotional Intelligence.* New York: Boston: Harvard Business School Press, 2002.

Lyubomirsky, Sonja. *The How of Happiness: A Scientific Approach to Getting the Life You Want.* New York, NY; Penguin Press, 2008.

Newberg, Andrew and Mark Robert Waldman. "Words Can Change Your Brain," *Psychology Today*, 2012.

The Arbinger Institute. *The Anatomy of Peace: Resolving the Heart of Conflict.* San Francisco, CA, Berrett-Koehler Publishers, 2006.

Whitworth, Laura, Karen Kimsey-House, Henry Kimsey-House and Phillip Sandahl. *Co-Active Coaching: New Skills for Coaching People Toward Success in Work and Life*, Second Edition. Mountain View, CA, 2007.

Zander, Benjamin and Rosamund Stone Zander. *The Art of*

Possibility: Transforming Professional and Personal Life.
Boston: Harvard Business School Press, 2000.

Zukav, Gary. *The Seat of the Soul.* New York: Simon and
Schuster, 1999.

ABOUT THE AUTHOR

Sara Smith, MCC, is a sought-after speaker, consultant and executive coach. Before beginning her work in sports, she spent nearly 30 years with IBM – in sales, then as an executive coach, consultant and professional change agent.

After leaving IBM, Sara worked with executives teaching emotional intelligence, leadership and how to lead organizational change. Her clients include IBM, Schneider Electric, Luminant Energy, PerkinElmer, Bonnell Aluminum and the University of North Texas.

Sara combined her love of coaching, leadership and emotional intelligence with a passion for sports when she wrote *Coach to Coach: Emotional Intelligence and Leadership for Winning Coaches.* She has worked with schools in the southwest including the University of Houston and the University of North Texas. Watch for her next book that teaches coaches how to create healthy, high function organizations.

Sara has taught EI and coaching skills to MBA students in the SMU Cox School of Business and doctoral students at Phillips Theological Seminary and Brite Divinity School.

Sara earned her bachelor and masters degrees from Texas Christian University. She is a Master Certified Coach (MCC) through the International Coach Federation.

Would you like to know about how to leverage emotional intelligence, leadership and coaching skills in your organization? Do you know others who can benefit from *Coach to Coach*? Hire Sara Smith to deliver the keynote at your next conference. You might also want Sara to coach you professionally to take your game to the next level.

Sara speaks before associations, teams and conferences. She offers talks and tailored seminars to fit your sport, players and staff. She will also coach you to speed your development as an emotionally intelligent coach. If you would like more information, call 817-924-0670 or make your request online at www.coachtocoach.info. You can email Sara directly at Sara@CoachtoCoach.info